CAMBRIDGE
UNIVERSITY PRESS

University Printing House, Cambridge CB2 8BS, United Kingdom

One Liberty Plaza, 20th Floor, New York, NY 10006, USA

477 Williamstown Road, Port Melbourne, VIC 3207, Australia

314–321, 3rd Floor, Plot 3, Splendor Forum, Jasola District Centre,
New Delhi – 110025, India

103 Penang Road, #05–06/07, Visioncrest Commercial, Singapore 238467

Cambridge University Press is part of the University of Cambridge.

It furthers the University's mission by disseminating knowledge in the pursuit of
education, learning, and research at the highest international levels of excellence.

www.cambridge.org
Information on this title: www.cambridge.org/9781009227483
DOI: 10.1017/9781009227490

First published 2022

A catalogue record for this publication is available from the British Library.

ISBN 978-1-009-22748-3 Paperback
ISSN 2514-3573 (online)
ISSN 2514-3581 (print)

Cambridge Elements ⁼

Elements in Evolutionary Economics
edited by
John Foster
University of Queensland
Jason Potts
RMIT University

INDUSTRIAL POLICY

The Coevolution of Public and Private Sources of Finance for Important Emerging and Evolving Technologies

Kenneth I. Carlaw
University of British Columbia–Okanagan

Richard G. Lipsey
Simon Fraser University

CAMBRIDGE
UNIVERSITY PRESS

Industrial Policy

The Coevolution of Public and Private Sources of Finance for Important Emerging and Evolving Technologies

Elements in Evolutionary Economics

DOI: 10.1017/9781009227490
First published online: June 2022

Kenneth I. Carlaw
University of British Columbia–Okanagan

Richard G. Lipsey
Simon Fraser University

Author for correspondence: Kenneth I. Carlaw, Kenneth.carlaw@ubc.ca

Abstract: Dismissing industrial policy because 'governments cannot pick winners' is counterproductive. This Element studying selected major innovations illustrates the fact that virtually all major new technologies have been developed by a synergetic cooperation between the public and the private sectors, each doing what it can do best. By examining how research and development (R&D) is financed, rather than where it takes place, the authors show that the role of the public sector is much more pronounced than is often thought. The nature of the cooperation – who does what – varies with the nature of each innovation so that simple, one-size-fits-all rules about what each sector should do are suspect. These results are particularly important because they challenge the scepticism in the United States and elsewhere about the importance of industrial policy, a scepticism that threatens to undermine the long-term and necessary cooperation between the public and private sectors in promoting growth-inducing innovations.

Keywords: industrial policy, coevolution, public finance, picking winners, innovation, technology

JEL classifications: L31, L33, L5, L6, O3

ISBNs: 9781009227483 (PB), 9781009227490 (OC)
ISSNs: 2514-3573 (online), 2514-3581 (print)

Contents

1 Introduction

The economy is an evolving system whose modern output trajectory has consistently shown trend growth, at least since the First Industrial Revolution that began in the mid eighteenth century.[*] Economic historians agree that technological change is the main driving force for this growth. Without it, growth would soon approach zero, ushering in what the Classical economists called the stationary state – the end of economic evolution. Joseph Schumpeter saw the entrepreneur as the main agent of technological change. However, finance is a necessary enabler of the actions of entrepreneurial agents, whether they are individuals or members of larger organisations.

Our concern in this Element is with the sources of the finance that enables technological evolution. Specifically, we ask: to what extent does the financing come from profit-oriented firms and individuals in what can be broadly called the private, for-profit sector, or from others who are not primarily profit oriented, located in what we call the not-for-profit sector? To this end, we divide all sources of financing into two groups: the for-profit sector (FPS) and the not-for-profit sector (NPS). We investigate the roles that agents in each sector have played, both directly and indirectly, in financing the creation and evolution of twelve major technologies that were innovated between the late nineteenth and early twenty-first centuries, many of which have been labelled general purpose technologies (GPTs).[1] We describe the development of our selected technologies in considerable detail, gathering from disparate sources many things that are already well known. Doing so emphasises four things that are not obvious in many discussions of industrial policy: (i) the extent to which agents in the NPS and FPS provided the necessary finance, sometimes in isolation from and sometimes in cooperation with each other; (ii) both the variety and the timing of the support that NPS agents have given to the technologies examined here; (iii) both the unexpected successes and failures that agents in both the NPS and FPS have encountered because they are dealing with inherent uncertainty; and (iv) that new knowledge does not diffuse instantly and costlessly throughout the whole economy. Studies of *the physical location* of research and development (R&D), inventions, and innovations typically give heavy weight to the FPS and

---

[*] This is a revised version of a paper presented to the Schumpeter Society conference in Jena, Germany, July 2014. We gratefully acknowledge funding support from SSHRC grant 410-2008-0726 and from CIGI grant 2881; helpful comments from Clifford Bekar, Ross Hickey, John Janmaat, Joanna Lipsey, Mohsen Javdani, and students of Economics 339 at UBC Okanagan; and research assistance from Stephanie Broder, Wendy Foster, Jennifer Lazarof, Colin McLean, Mitchel Naito, and Jennifer Watt.
[1] The method of qualitative analysis employed here is referred to as 'appreciative theorizing' by Nelson and Winter (1982) and is related to process tracing used by social science researchers who deal with qualitative data (e.g., Befani and Mayne (2018)).

much less weight to the NPS. However, when we study the sources of *the finance* that enabled these technological developments, this greatly increases the relative weight attached to the NPS compared with that of the FPS.

Section 2 considers how two views of the economy, the Neoclassical and the evolutionary, influence attitudes to public-sector support for technological inventions and innovations.

Section 3 deals with some preliminary concepts and definitions. We distinguish four trajectories in the evolution of any new technology: the *invention trajectory* covers the scientific and technological developments that precede the emergence of an identifiable technology; the *efficiency trajectory* is the time path of the cost of producing a unit of the service provided by the technology; the *applications trajectory* is comprised of the technological products, processes, and forms of organisation that depend on it; the *diffusion trajectory* is the spread of the technology to uses in other places and other times, both nationally and internationally. For each of these trajectories in each of our twelve technologies we indicate which developments were financed mainly by the NPS, mainly by the FPS, or, as is often the case, by some combination of both.

Section 4 gives a detailed analysis of the major technologies that we have studied, together with some lessons that we derive from each case study. We divide our technologies into five main groups (groups that were discerned after completing our case studies rather than being imposed a priori): Group 1, *little NPS support except for the applications trajectory*, the internal combustion engine; Group 2, *NPS support mainly for the invention trajectory*, refrigeration; Group 3, *NPS support mainly for the efficiency, applications, and diffusion trajectories*, railways, automobiles, aircraft, and agriculture; Group 4, *NPS support mainly for the invention and efficiency trajectories*, the iron steamship; Group 5, *NPS support for all trajectories*, electricity, computers, the Internet, and lasers.

Section 5 presents more general lessons that apply to most or all of the technologies. Two examples follow. First, the more a technology depends on science, the larger the place for NPS support for the relevant trajectories. Second, major technologies have significant coevolutionary complementarities among themselves. As a result, NPS support in the development trajectories of any one technology has significant positive and often impossible-to-foresee impacts on the development trajectories of other technologies, including some that were not directly supported by the NPS themselves. Investments from the NPS can also help to create positive feedbacks through these indirect impacts by creating further complementarities that subsequently operate on the originally supported technology. Thus, calculations of the return to NPS support for a particular technology typically underestimate that return unless they account for the impact on the entire interconnected, complementary system.

When we began our study, we had no strong view on the sources of financing other than the general feeling that the public sector might be a more important source than is often acknowledged in popular debates about industrial policy. We were surprised, therefore, to discover just how important public sector finance has been and how interrelated it has been with private-sector finance in most of our cases. We conclude in Section 6 that dismissing industrial policy with statements such as 'governments cannot pick winners' relies on an empty slogan to avoid detailed consideration of the actual complicated, multifaceted relationships between the private and public sectors in encouraging the inventions and innovations that are the root of economic growth.

2 Policy Implications of Two Views of the Economy

2.1 The Neoclassical View

The Neoclassical view holds that the place of the NPS is to provide a level playing field and remove market imperfections, leaving the FPS to generate an efficient allocation of resources and an optimum amount of economic growth. An important class of market imperfections arises from externalities, often called third-party effects. These are measurable benefits (positive externalities) and costs (negative externalities) conferred by an initiating agent on others. They are effects that the initiating agent has no incentive to consider and, in the case of beneficial new technological knowledge, are usually assumed to be costlessly and instantaneously conferred across all agents. These can be offset in principle by imposing on the initiator a tax equal to the cost, or a subsidy equal to the benefit, that they confer on others. Kenneth Arrow (1962) points out one important source of (net) positive externalities, the introduction of generally available new products and processes. These externalities result in a suboptimal amount of R&D. This provides a reason for the NPS to subsidise R&D to ensure that the amount gets closer to the social optimum. Assuming that the decision environment is characterised only by risk rather than by uncertainty, the FPS will optimise by equating the expected marginal products of all lines of R&D. The NPS role that is then justified is a generalised and hence 'non-distorting' support given equally to all R&D (as a subsidy or tax relief).[2]

---

[2] This view was upset long ago by 'The General Theory of Second Best' (Lipsey and Lancaster 1958), which shows that if all market imperfections cannot be removed or compensated for, there is no presumption that removing any one of these will raise the value of whatever social objective function is being considered.

2.2 The Evolutionary View

One intellectual basis for supporting NPS activities that go beyond what is sanctioned in the Neoclassical view is found in the evolutionary view of the economy. Without going into detail here, this view emphasises three important aspects of the economy: (i) pervasive uncertainty; (ii) that new knowledge does not, as assumed in Neoclassical economics, diffuse instantly and costlessly through the economy, as is shown in many of the cases described in what follows such as early aircraft-related research, the Korean electronics industry and Korea's adoption of lean production techniques; and (iii) the endogeneity of both technological change[3] and, at least to some extent, scientific research.[4]

The fact that inventions and innovations are fraught with uncertainties upsets the idea that the private sector will (with the appropriate, generalised NPS support for R&D) allocate resources, including R&D, in a socially optimal way.

> Research into technological change (see especially Rosenberg 1982, 1994 and 1996) establishes that uncertainty is always present and often pervasive in the search for new technological knowledge. One cannot even enumerate the possible outcomes of various lines of R&D devoted to inventing and innovating some new technology. Large sums are sometimes spent with no positive results, while trivial expenditures sometimes produce results of great value. Furthermore, the search for one objective often produces results relevant to different objectives. (Lipsey, 2013: 44)

Thus, rather than maximising the expected value of profit from all lines of activity, including R&D, firms should be seen as groping into an uncertain future in a profit-oriented but not profit-maximising manner. Indeed, as the detailed discussions of our technologies illustrate, all agents, regardless of sector and motivation, who seek to effect technological change should be regarded as groping into an uncertain future.

The fact that technological change is endogenous (influenced by actions in both the FPS and the NPS) undermines the view that the socially optimal policy action is to allocate resources efficiently *given the current state of technology* – as the Scottish-born Canadian economist John Rae (1905) pointed out long ago.

Since it denies the existence of a unique optimum allocation of resources to all activities, including R&D, the evolutionary view opens the way for an empirical evaluation of the pros and cons of specific actions by both the NPS and FPS to encourage technological change and economic growth.

---

[3] Popularized by Joseph Schumpeter (1942) and documented by many economic historians long before it was introduced into macro models by Lucas (1988) and Romer (1990).

[4] Argued persuasively in Rosenberg (1982, chapter 7).

2.3 Spillovers

Another reason for the conclusion just stated lies in the existence of spillovers, a concept that includes but goes well beyond externalities. Carlaw and Lipsey (2002) provide a definition of technological complementarities that enables the distinction of spillovers that are externalities from those that are not.

> A *technological complementarity* arises in any situation in which the past or present decisions of the initiating agents with respect to their own technologies affect the value of the receiving agents' existing technologies and/or their opportunities for making further technological changes.
>
> (p. 1310)

Of course, the initiating and receiving agents may be identical, as when an agent's technological innovation affects the value of that agent's other technologies. Here we confine ourselves to the cases in which the two agents are separate entities. While the aforementioned complementarity refers to technical relations, *spillovers* refer to economic relations, occurring when technological complementarities provide profitable opportunities for agents to exploit previously created technological knowledge. Some spillovers are externalities in the sense that they provide what are at the time identifiable and (at least in principle) measurable benefits to the receiving agents. Others, however, go well beyond externalities, conferring benefits on subsequent agents that may extend over times and spaces that cannot even be identified, let alone measured, at the time of the initiating event.

As our case studies reveal, technological complementarities pervade human-created economic systems of technological innovation, production, and trade. Carlaw and Lipsey (2002) point out that although these technological complementarities drive Arrow-style externalities, where a calculable rate of return exists for a third party, others take the form of opportunities to create novel products, processes, and organisational structures that would not have existed in absence of the originating technology. These spillovers can persist for decades, even centuries. For one example, electricity created both the opportunities for all the gadgets that revolutionised household operations in the first half of the twentieth century and the technologies that created the modern information and communications technology (ICT) revolution, such as telephones, telegraphs, radios, TVs, faxes, electric lighting, computers, email, the Internet, and satellite signals. For another example, the computer in its various forms has been incorporated in a massive number of technologies, including aircraft controls, the Global Positioning System (GPS), automated factories, mobile phones, myriad electronic games, and the Internet, to mention just a few. Similar comments can be made about the laser and many other science-based modern technologies. In all these cases, those who were responsible for the invention and early development of the technology could not have foreseen its many future applications, let alone gain a compensation equal to even a small fraction of the economic value those applications enabled.

The absence of obvious monetary incentives to the original inventors and innovators commensurate with all the economic gains that they will create now and in the future provides a reason for the NPS to support these activities when the spillovers can be at least dimly appreciated, even if not identifiable in detail. Note that by covering all spillovers, this conclusion goes further than Arrow's classic justification for subsidising R&D, which only applies to identifiable externalities.

Although NPS actors are subject to the same uncertainties as FPS agents with respect to identifying spillovers, they typically have different motivations and risk/uncertainty tolerances than FPS agents. Therefore, the two sets of agents can play different (complementary) roles in the financing of the evolutionary development of technological complementarities and exploitation of the spillovers they create.

2.4 Summary

Neoclassical policy advice is quite simple and quite general (as long as we ignore second best), applying to all countries whatever their current circumstances: remove market imperfections wherever they are found. In contrast, evolutionary advice is context dependent, there being no simple set of policy rules that apply to all countries, all times, and all circumstances. Participation of the NPS is warranted in the presence of the pervasive uncertainty and massive spillovers that accompany endogenous R&D designed to advance technological knowledge.

3 Concepts and Definitions

At the outset, we need to make some important distinctions and define some terms, many of which are borrowed from Lipsey, Carlaw, and Bekar (2005), hereafter LCB.

3.1 Technology and Structure

Key concepts dealt with in this section are 'technology' and the underlying structure of the economy, which LCB call the 'facilitating structure'. Technology is defined as follows (LCB, 2005: 58):

> [T]echnological knowledge, technology for short, is the set of ideas specifying all activities that create economic value. It comprises: (1) knowledge

about product technologies, the specifications of everything that is produced; (2) knowledge about process technologies, the specifications of all processes by which goods and services are produced; (3) knowledge about organizational technologies, the specification of how activity is organized in productive and administrative units for producing present and future goods and services (which thus includes knowledge about how to conduct R&D).

This concept of technology distinguishes it from its physical embodiment in capital goods. A particular machine is often referred to in popular discussion as a technology, but the technology is the knowledge of how to make that machine, not the machine itself. Given the knowledge, a competent agent can make the machine; given the machine, the agent might not be able to reverse-engineer it to discover the technological knowledge that went into creating it.

The separation of technologies from their physical embodiments leads to the following definition. *The facilitating structure* is the set of realisations of technological knowledge – that is, the actual physical objects, people, structures, and organisational forms in which technological knowledge is embodied.[5] This separation is important because the evolution of major new technologies is strongly influenced by how well they fit into the existing facilitating structure. Some require large and persistent changes in that structure, while others fit almost seamlessly into it.

3.2 Evolutionary Trajectories

We identify four trajectories that are distinct in principle but sometimes so intertwined that they cannot be dealt with separately in practice.

The *invention trajectory* begins with all the scientific and technological developments that precede the emergence of an identifiable technology. Since new technological knowledge evolves continually, it is somewhat arbitrary to state exactly when the invention stage is over. It may roughly be thought of as ending when 'proof of concept' is established. For example, in the case of electricity, this trajectory lasted several hundred years including Gilbert's *de Magneta* in 1600, but having precedents in magnetism dating back much further and ending with the first useful electricity that was not generated by a storage battery.

---

[5] The structure includes (1) all physical capital; (2) consumers' durables and residential housing; (3) people, who they are, where they live, and all human capital that resides in them and that is related to productive activities, including tacit knowledge of how to operate existing value-creating facilities; (4) the actual physical organisation of production facilities, including labour practices; (5) the managerial and financial organisation of firms; (6) the geographical location of productive activities; (7) industrial concentration; (8) all infrastructure; (9) all private-sector financial institutions and instruments; (10) government-owned industries; (11) educational institutions; (12) all research units whether in the public or the private sector (LCB, 2005: 60–1).

The *efficiency trajectory* of a technology is the time path of the cost of producing a unit of the service provided by the technology. When more than one service is provided, it is an index of the multidimensional array of the costs of these various services.

The *applications trajectory* of a technology is composed of the technological products, processes, and forms of organisation that depend on it – as the electric washing machine depends on electricity – or include it, in one form or another – as when a computer is embedded in a robot.

The *diffusion trajectory* is the spread of the technology to uses in other places, as when computer use spread from the scientific lab to the office and from the countries where it was invented to the rest of the world.

Several points need to be noted about these trajectories.

First, diffusion is often associated with major new applications (e.g., computers and the Internet, or lasers and barcoding for scanning). Because this trajectory is so intimately related to the applications trajectory, we treat these two trajectories together as the applications-diffusion trajectory in what follows.

Second, the evolution of the invention and the efficiency and applications-diffusion trajectories can sometimes be divided into a *pre-commercial* stage, when developments are public property, and a *commercial* stage, when developments can be appropriated privately.

Third, where the various trajectories are distinct and follow different paths, the failure to distinguish among them has been the cause of much confusion in the literature concerning the evolution of and the FPS and NPS support for new technologies.

3.3 Agents

We divide agents into two broad groups: those in the FPS and those in the NPS. This second group is subdivided into two groups, agents in non-governmental organisations (NGOs) and those in the public policy sector (PPS). Those in the latter sector are in turn subdivided into two groups according to their objectives, those that primarily seek economic objectives (EOs) and those that seek non-economic objectives (NEOs). Figure 1 summarises:

The FPS includes individuals and organisations operating in pursuit of market incentives such as profits, sales, management earnings, or other similar economic objectives, which we call collectively *economic returns*. These are the agents that inhabit any standard textbook on microeconomic theory.

The NPS includes all other agents, but we confine our attention to those whose activities affect, either directly or indirectly, the evolution of technologies in their

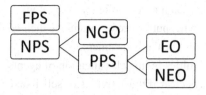

Figure 1 Agent type

invention, efficiency, and applications-diffusion trajectories. Sometimes we treat this sector as a whole but at other times it is useful to consider its subdivisions.

The NGOs include both agents in NGOs and those whose activities are not motivated by a search for profits. We refer to these agents collectively as being in NGOs. They are motivated by such non-monetary incentives as pure curiosity, philanthropy, the pursuit of knowledge, or personal prestige. Their activities, however, create opportunities (and influence evolutionary trajectories) either directly or indirectly, in some cases allowing others to make economic returns. This group includes those in privately funded, not-for-profit, educational institutions (in the United States, some hospitals and educational facilities are for-profit institutions), the church, and privately funded bodies dedicated to the pursuit of scientific and technological advancement, such as the Royal Society and various professional organisations. Many of the agents we consider were educated in schools and universities that were wholly or partially publicly funded. The activities we study had significant NGO support to the extent that these agents' human capital assisted them. We acknowledge this here once and for all and do not go into the educational background of the agents when their contributions are studied.

The public policy sector: this second subcategory of the NPS can be subdivided into two groups distinguished by motivations. The EO includes publicly funded organisations that pursue policies to achieve economic objectives, either directly through scientific and/or technological advance or indirectly, as when the facilitating structure is altered by such means as building roads or contributing to the health and education of workers. The EO includes: (i) government departments and other government-financed and directed bodies, (ii) all government granting bodies such as the National Science Foundation, (iii) quasi-independent bodies that are financed by governments but not directed by them in their day-to-day activities, (iv) educational institutions, to the extent that they are financed by governments whether or not they are independent of government policy. The second subcategory of the PPS includes those concerned with achieving NEOs that will benefit themselves, such as military power or election victories. Their activities in pursuit of these objectives often have technological spin-offs that either allow others in the private sector to achieve economic returns – for example, when a new military technology has commercial spin-offs – or allow others in the public sector to achieve their goals that in turn affect scientific and/or technological advancement.

We note some difficulties in this classification of agents.

First, it is not always clear if the activities of self-financed individual agents fall within the NGOs or the FPS. For example, did agents who sought fame for scientific discoveries but subsequently patented and profited from them start in an NGO and move into the FPS, or were they really in the FPS from the outset? Barring much psychological knowledge about motivations, it is often impossible to tell. Fortunately, when the agents were financed by an outside body, it is usually possible to tell if the financing came from either the FPS or the NPS, which is our main concern.

Second, the boundary between NGOs and the PPS on one hand and the FPS on the other hand is clear enough since the members of the first two groups are not pursuing economic returns that will accrue directly to themselves. However, the boundary between NGOs and the PPS is neither clear nor invariant over time. For example, the PPS and NGOs currently shade into each other as privately funded universities have come increasingly to rely on government funds to finance research as well as other university activities. Although we are interested in distinguishing between the financing that comes from the PPS and from NGOs, it is the clearer division between the FPS and the NPS financing that is most important to us.

Third, by far the most important ambiguity concerns where the boundary lies *within* one major agent – for example, Bell Laboratories – rather than with the general boundary *between* any of our main sectors. The Appendix gives a short outline of some key facts about Bell Labs. These pose a problem for us in that, although its work was mainly financed by AT&T at its inception, the research became increasingly dependent on government financing during and after World War II. It is possible to locate specific funding grants from outside Bell Labs in some cases but not others. In the latter cases, it is unclear whether the financing was fully NPS, FPS, or both.

3.4 Objectives

To document the extent to which technologies have been financed by either or both the FPS and the NPS, we study the evolutionary trajectories for the development of a group of major technologies that came into widespread use sometime after the first half of the nineteenth century. Although our analyses are mostly qualitative, we believe that they throw considerable light on the significant role of the NPS in many of the major technological developments over this period. Indeed, our results challenge the view commonly stated either explicitly or implicitly in economic theory textbooks, that the FPS is the only major force behind the technological evolution that has continually transformed economies over the past several centuries. Once it is established that both the FPS and the NPS have played major parts in that evolution, other questions arise, such as: what are the conditions in which NPS interventions are likely to be either successful and/or beneficial or unsuccessful and/or harmful? These issues are left for another paper (Lipsey and Carlaw, 2020).

The following table groups the technologies that we consider in this Element into five categories depending on which of the trajectories received significant NPS support. We did not choose the technologies we study in this Element to fit into the categories of the table. Rather these technologies were chosen as a selection (not exhaustive) of technologies that had major economic impact in the late nineteenth and twentieth centuries. The organisational categories of the table emerged as we studied for each technology how NPS support was involved with its development trajectories.

4 Case Studies

We now consider our case studies divided into the groups defined in Table 1.

4.1 GROUP 1: Little NPS Support except for the Applications Trajectory

4.1.1 Internal Combustion Engine

The internal combustion engine is the culmination of a cluster of technologies that incorporate the basic principle of generating inanimate power by igniting combustible material in a confined space to release energy. This principle has been fundamental in enabling and/or enhancing several critically important nineteenth- and twentieth-century technologies as their power source (e.g., motor vehicles and aircraft).

Invention Trajectory

The first commercially successful internal combustion engine was created by Samuel Brown in London between 1823 and 1833.[6] The first free-piston engine was developed by Eugenio Barsanti and Felice Mattucci between 1854 and 1864 in Italy, but it was a commercial failure.[7] In 1860, Etienne Lenoir

---

[6] *The Repertory of Patent Inventions: And Other Discoveries and Improvements* (1825: 439).

[7] A free-piston engine requires the piston to be disconnected from the output shaft on the upstroke and so was not a practical design for many applications of the internal combustion engine (McNeil, 2002: 305).

Table 1 Significant Not-For-Profit (NPS) Assistance

	Invention trajectory	Efficiency trajectory	Applications-diffusion trajectories
GROUP 1			
Internal combustion engine			Yes
GROUP 2			
Refrigeration	Yes		
GROUP 3			
Railways		Yes	Yes
Automobiles		Yes	Yes
Aircraft		Yes	Yes
Agriculture		Yes	Yes
GROUP 4			
Iron steamships	Yes	Yes	
GROUP 5			
Electricity	Yes	Yes	Yes
Computers	Yes	Yes	Yes
Internet	Yes	Yes	Yes
Lasers	Yes	Yes	Yes

produced 'the first internal combustion engine that could be said to provide a reliable and continuous source of power' (McNeil, 2002: 303–5). Nonetheless, the invention trajectory did not get past the stage of ad hoc trial and error until 1862 when Alphonse Bearu de Rochas laid out the full theory of how an internal combustion engine works. Then, in 1876, Nikolaus Otto invented the first successful four-stroke gasoline (in gaseous form) engine (Bellis, 2018). In spite of its great weight and fuel inefficiency, making it useful for only stationary applications, it was successful commercially and sold fifty thousand units over the next seventeen years. Finally, in 1884, Gottlieb Daimler and Wilhelm Maybach developed the first successful high-power lightweight engine. Their invention of the carburettor (much disputed in patent litigation) enabled the engine to use liquid gasoline.[8] Its high power-to-weight ratio allowed it to be applied in a much larger variety of technologies than Otto's engine (including locomotion). The internal combustion, gasoline-powered engine had arrived.

---

[8] In Britain, Edward Butler had invented and patented a liquid petroleum carburettor of a slightly different design in 1884.

The other main form of the internal combustion engine was invented by Rudolf Diesel, who took out patents for his device in 1892 and 1893. The engine was simpler than Daimler's because the heat and high pressure within the cylinder on its compression stroke ignited the fuel on its own without any need for a carefully timed spark to set it off. Because of the need for high pressure in its cylinders, the engine was heavier than the gasoline engine and so not as versatile. After difficulties with the use of coal dust as a fuel, diesel oil was used and the diesel engine was created in more or less its present form.

All these activities were undertaken by individuals in search of profits and without discernable NPS assistance.

The Efficiency and Applications-Diffusion Trajectories

A succession of small inventions and adaptions increased the efficiency of both gasoline and diesel engines over the early years of their use. For example, with gasoline engines, the introduction of supercharging techniques by Dugald Clerk in 1878 significantly increased the power-to-weight ratio. Early gasoline engines suffered from a 'detonation' or 'knock' problem, which occurs when fuel ignites in the engine earlier than it should. This problem was solved by the discovery of tetraethynol as a fuel additive by researchers at General Motors in 1921, which enabled the modern high-compression engine with spark ignition (McNeil, 2002: 315–17). These developments were all financed by agents in the FPS.

The diesel engine was used in submarines during World War I and in many stationary applications such as generating electricity where it was not otherwise available. Because of its much higher power-to-weight ratio, the gasoline engine was used in most transportation devices, cars, trucks, busses, and soon in airplanes, where the development of supercharging raised the power-to-weight ratio enough to allow their more extensive use. Most of the direct applications of both of these types of engines were obvious to agents in the FPS from the outset and hence the financing came from this sector.

Some of the major applications of the internal combustion engine were supported by the PPS, particularly in military applications – the diesel engine for the submarine and the gasoline engine for the airplane are examples. Many of these applications also required a substantial infrastructure before they could be fully exploited. For instance, there was major PPS support for the development of road, rail, and airport infrastructure. We treat several of these applications as separate major technologies subsequently, although they would not have occurred without the internal combustion engine.

Lessons

1. Although the invention, efficiency, and applications-diffusion trajectories of a new technology may be obvious and commercially viable from the outset, as they were with the internal combustion engine, the full development of these trajectories may require the development of other technologies that incorporate the original one. If these, in turn, require NPS finance, that support may be indirectly needed for the full development of the initial technology.

2. Since applications, diffusion, and improvements typically coevolve, the PPS-financed infrastructure that allows a technology's full exploitation may also lead to further improvements in the efficiency of that technology. Although these developments may be carried out by the FPS, they would not have been attempted without the PPS provision of the infrastructure. Such was the case with the internal combustion engine.

4.2 GROUP 2: NPS Support for the Invention Trajectory

4.2.1 Refrigeration

The technology of refrigeration has its roots in human history as far back as the preservation of food, but the intentional creation of chemical-mechanical cooling began in the eighteenth century with the development of the relevant scientific principles. Refrigeration has enabled the control of temperature in closed environments, especially for the transportation and storage of perishable goods.

Invention Trajectory

The invention trajectory of refrigeration came initially from individuals, many of whom were university professors in the NPS, specifically NGOs, while others financed their activities with their own funds. William Cullen, Benjamin Franklin, and John Hadley were almost certainly driven by scientific curiosity. Later contributors, especially those who patented their ideas, were probably driven by a mixture of curiosity and the search for commercial success.

In 1748, Cullen, who was a professor at the University of Glasgow, was the first to note that the evaporation of ethyl ether causes a fall in temperature and in 1755, he was able to make ice in a crude machine. Franklin and Hadley, a professor of chemistry at Cambridge University, showed in 1758 that the evaporation of liquids such as alcohol and ether could reduce the temperature of water below its freezing point. In 1805, Oliver Evans, an American engineer, proposed that the evaporation should take place in a vacuum. The next big improvement came in 1810 when Sir John Leslie, a professor at the University of Edinburgh, used a combination of water and sulphuric acid to increase the speed of freezing. In 1834, Jacob Perkins, an inventor/entrepreneur who had many patents for machines, used Evans' ideas to construct and patent a vapor-compression machine. John Gorrie made the first air cycle refrigerating machine that made ice in 1844. He applied for a British patent in 1850 and an American patent in 1851 (Thévenot, 1979).

Efficiency and Applications-Diffusion Trajectories

At this point, refrigeration moved into its efficiency and applications-diffusion phases and it is unclear whether these early developments were exclusively NPS or FPS supported.[9] Instead (as is a common theme throughout this study) there appears to have been a combination of support from NPS university-based inventors and FPS profit-motivated entrepreneurs. The ether refrigeration machine was improved upon by university professor Alexander C. Twining in 1850–3, by James Harrison in 1855, and by Ferdinand Carré, a French engineer, in 1857 (Thévenot, 1979). Beyond 1855, the development of refrigeration seems to have been exclusively FPS funded. In many cases, the commercially profitable applications, including the making of ice cream and beer, had been obvious to private individuals and firms from the earliest days and only awaited the invention of viable machines.

Refrigeration shares complementarities with the efficiency and applications-diffusion trajectories of many other technologies. Examples include such technologies as internal combustion engines embodied in the transportation technologies of railways, automobiles, agriculture, ships, and aircraft, where refrigeration allows the global transport of perishable goods and provides air conditioning for the comfort of passengers. It is complementary to a vast array of biomedical technologies, including those linked to organ and tissue transplant, human reproduction, blood and plasma storage, disease research and treatment, and so forth.

Lessons

1. When there is much uncertainty about the technology early on, as is often the case and was with refrigeration, certain practical components of it need to be demonstrated by agents in the NPS before those in the FPS can foresee profitable investments in the technology. In such cases, NPS support is needed early in the invention trajectory.

---

[9] A few initial developments were supported by NPS activity, but most of the subsequent development was FPS funded, so we do not include a "YES" in Table 1 for Efficiency and Applications-Diffusion.

2. If, as with refrigeration, there are many obvious commercial applications, once the basic principles have been proven, the invention, efficiency, and applications-diffusion trajectories can be readily financed by the FPS.
3. See also lesson 1 for railroads.

4.3 GROUP 3: NPS Support for the Efficiency and Applications Trajectories

4.3.1. Railroads

We use the term *railroads* to identify a complementary cluster of technologies that formed a transformative transportation technology in the late nineteenth century and throughout the twentieth. In railroads, we observe a theme common to the transportation technologies (railroads, iron steamships, automobiles, and aircraft) examined here. These typically comprise a complementary cluster of technologies – power, materials, mechanical, and communications – and usually require some form of supporting infrastructure. Railroads exhibit vivid examples of this complementarity of technologies. The power base of early railroads was the steam engine, which was originally invented to pump water out of coal mines from which rudimentary forms of railroad were being used to transport the coal. The steam-powered railway combined with materials (wood, iron, and steel) and information and communications technologies (public timekeeping and departure/arrival scheduling, and the telegraph) became an integrated system that worked in cooperation with other transport technologies (such as local trucking).

Invention Trajectory

The original railroads were carts operating on wooden railbeds used to haul coal out of mines as early as the start of the seventeenth century (Jones, 2012; King, 2010). The carts were moved first by hand, then by horse. Later, the railroads were extended to surface transport to move coal over short distances from the pit head to harbours and rivers. They were often constructed on a grade that allowed gravity to do much of the work. By 1800, there were extensive systems of railroads in England and other parts of Europe and United States that depended on either gravity or animal power and were totally financed by the FPS (Jones, 2012; King, 2010).

In the 1803, the FPS-funded British Surrey Iron Railway was the world's first railway open to the public. It was horse drawn and ran from Wandsworth to Croydon on a track of just more than eight miles. In 1804, the Oystermouth and Swansea Railway, originally designed to carry stone and later altered to carry passengers, opened. It continued to carry passengers until its closure in 1960 (Yorke, 2007: 12).

In 1800, James Watt's patent for the steam engine ran out and his refusal to contemplate high-pressure engines no longer had force (Boldrin and Levine, 2008). In 1804, Richard Trevithick made the breakthrough to a high-pressure engine that operated well above one atmosphere of pressure. It developed a much more favourable power-to-weight ratio than anything Watt had built (Crump, 2007) *and was thus suitable to being mounted on transportation equipment.* In the United States, Oliver Evans built the first American high-pressure engine, which he used on a dredge in the Philadelphia harbour (Hunter, 1985).

In 1813, the English engineer John Blenkinsopp built the first successful steam locomotive. It was used to move coal a short distance in Yorkshire. A year later, George Stephenson built a greatly improved engine. He followed this one with a succession of improved models, which soon incorporated his invention of the steam blast that sent smoke up the chimney and pulled air into the firebox (Lowe, 1989).

In 1821, Parliament authorised the building of a railway from Stockton to Darlington to haul coal and passengers. Using a mixture of horses and steam engines, the railway opened in 1825. It was FPS financed, mostly by investors who were local to the area, although the sale of public shares had to be approved by Parliament (Heavisides, 1912). Next came the Liverpool and Manchester railroad which was a cooperative NPS-FPS effort. It was financed by the FPS but used (NPS) parliamentary-approved issuance of shares, bonds, and mortgages. It was built and managed by a coalition of NPS and FPS entrepreneurs (businessmen, bankers, engineers, and politicians) who became the directors of the Railway (Donaghy, 1966; Pollins, 1952; Science and Industry Museum, 2018).[10] For the first time, steam was used exclusively to provide the locomotive power and Robert Stephenson's Rocket was selected to do the job (Burton, 1980; Casserley, 1960: 7–8). The engine used his latest invention, a boiler containing multiple tubes through which hot gasses from the furnace circulated through the water chamber to heat it efficiently. When that railway was opened in 1830 for both passenger and freight service, the invention trajectory of the railroad could be said to have been completed. The invention trajectory was FPS financed but that financing required PPS support. Further government approvals were often required for route access on lands for the railbeds.

---

[10] In this case, NPS and FPS interests were cooperatively tied together to create the railway (Science and Industry Museum (2018)).

Efficiency and Applications-Diffusion Trajectories

Efficiency continued to be increased by many further ancillary inventions and adaptations. Indeed, the development of steam-powered railroads resulted in a cascade of induced innovations noted by Rosenberg (1982: 69) that were almost exclusively FPS financed. It also set in motion several smaller innovations that increased the efficiency of railroads and were also FPS financed. 'The technological sources of productivity growth included a series of important inventions specific to the railroads – air brakes[11] and automatic couplers – the substitution of steel for iron rails,[12] and the gradual improvement in the design of locomotives and rolling stock." (Rosenberg, 1982: 69). These were financed by FPS agents. Major increases in efficiency continue to this day, especially those for high-speed passenger trains including electromagnetic systems, tunnelling technology, methods for dealing with grades, and bridging technology.

Britain and Europe

Because the obvious economic value of railways was soon realised after the technology had been proven by private FPS entrepreneurs, in Britain and Europe the development of railways remained largely supported by FPS investment (Hijiya, 1973). The only PPS role was through Acts of Parliament authorising both the incorporation of a rail company and the construction of specific routes with funds raised by investors.

During World War I, various British railways were either taken over by the Government or heavily subsidised out of national funds (Macassey, 1922). After the war, wanting to return the system to private ownership and restore the level of efficiency that had been greatly reduced by the wartime operations, the government passed the Railways Acts of 1919 and 1921. These reorganised all of the railways in Great Britain into four groups; the Acts adapted a new basis of rates and charges; and created "a great conciliation machinery for the settlement, as between railway companies and their employees, to all questions relating to hours of work, rates of wages, and conditions of employment" (Macassey, 1922). To clear outstanding claims from the wartime agreements between the railways and government, the government made a single payment of £60,000,000 (Channon, 1981). From that time until 1947, when they were nationalised by the Labour government, the railways were in private hands but

---

[11] Air brakes were invented and patented by George Westinghouse in 1869, who then founded the Westinghouse Air Brake manufacturing company in Pennsylvania.

[12] In 1890, the Pennsylvania Railroad, an FPS company, was among the first to employ steel rails (Fishlow, 1966).

under heavy government regulation, which included the Railways (Agreement) Act, 1935, that made available a PPS-funded loan of £26·5 million for railway modernisation and the Railway Rates Tribunal which reviewed railway efficiency and provided annual reports into the mid 1930s (Savage (2006):154–9).

Elsewhere

The PPS provided much support for the development of railways in the United States, Canada, Australia, and Japan. In the first three cases, this had much to do with lack of apparent commercial viability due to the large geographic area and the relatively low population density dispersed across the expansive geography (Hood, 2006: 20). However, in all four cases, the support was mainly due to political motivations.

Around 1805, the first railroad constructed in the United States was supported entirely by the FPS and operated on Boston's Beacon Hill (Gamst, 1992). One example of mixed support was the Baltimore & Ohio Railroad (B&O), which was an FPS enterprise whose development was supported by PPS funding at both the municipal and state levels (Previts & Samson, 2000). Although this railway was only marginally successful as a private FPS company, it did create many social spillovers, particularly for landowners and farmers along its route (Previts & Samson, 2000). Between 1830 and 1840, railroad mileage in America increased from 73 to 3,328 (Hijiya, 1973). This expansion was funded by a combination of the FPS and PPS. The latter typically funded what were perceived as routes that were insufficiently profitable but with significant social pay-off (Cootner, 1963).

By the end of the 1830s, states such as Massachusetts, Pennsylvania, Virginia, South Carolina, Georgia, and a few Western states in the United States had allocated large sums for railroad construction, often through the issuance of public bonds. 'The cost of the extensive east-west projects was too great, their profits too uncertain, to attract private capital. If they were to be built at all, they had to be financed by public loans based on a state's ability to tax rather than by private loans based on a corporation's ability to pay' (Chandler, 1990: 249). The shorter, more predictably profitable north-south lines were for the most part privately funded. Land grants occurred between 1850 and 1871 (Cochrane, 1993). By 1930, these grants totalled 179 million acres coming from both the states and the federal government. Of these, 77 per cent went to transcontinental lines, with the remainder going to regional Midwestern and Southern railways (Mercer, 1982).

The Champlain-St. Lawrence Railroad of 1836, the first railroad built in Canada, was financed by a group of merchants. It and some other small, early railroads financed by the FPS were not commercially successful. Major PPS support came with the passing of the Railway Guarantee Act of 1849. This made railway companies eligible for support on bond interest payments once half the line was completed. Also, the Municipal Loan Act of 1852 allowed towns to borrow at a preferential rate based on the credit rating of the Province of Upper Canada through a consolidated Municipal Loans Fund managed by the government of the province.[13] The boom that followed resulted in many failures, the largest being the Grand Trunk Railway (GTR), which had been partly funded by the federal government through cash and land grants, guaranteed interest rates, and rebates (Marsh, 2009). It was bailed out twice via the Grand Trunk Arraignments Acts, first in 1862 and then in 1872 (Lukasiewicz, 1976). The GTR eventually went bankrupt in 1919 and was taken over by the Canadian federal government, which up to that time had loaned the GTR CA\$28 million. The Canadian National Railway (CNR) took over its management in 1923 (Currie, 1957).

The Canadian Pacific Railway (CPR) was founded primarily because of political concerns about preventing the West from being settled and annexed by the United States and bringing British Columbia into the Dominion of Canada with only small regard for economic considerations (McDougall, 1968: 12–18). Private groups were unable to secure sufficient funding and the GTR declined to participate. Canadian government representatives negotiated in London and Ottawa with British financier groups for funding, eventually making a deal that led to legislation establishing the CPR. The government provided it with funding, land, duty-free material imports, and monopoly rights for twenty years (McDougall, 1968: 40–1).

In 1917, the Intercolonial, the Canadian Northern, the National Transcontinental, and the Grand Trunk Pacific (successor to the GTR) Railways were heavily indebted to British banks, and access to capital disappeared during World War I. Under the threat of failure, the Canadian federal government amalgamated and nationalised these companies to become the CNR (Tucker, 2009). Funding for the establishment and operation of the Intercolonial Railway of Canada, which later became part of the CNR, was provided by the federal government and the government of Nova Scotia as part of Confederation (Waite, 1962). The Canadian Northern Railway had been created in the FPS from some minor branch lines in Manitoba, but it was assisted in its development by means such as bond guarantees from

---

[13] The borrowing occurred before any money was placed in the 'fund' and was underwritten by the speculation that the repayments from the municipalities would balance the fund's liabilities. In the end, \$3 million of unpaid municipal debt was rolled into the Canadian public debt (British North America Legislative Database, 1852).

several western provinces (Regehr, 1972). The National Transcontinental Railway was a government-financed railway running from Moncton to Winnipeg which later became part of the CNR agglomeration in 1918 (Regehr, 2006).

In Australia, in 1904, less than 4.5 per cent of more than fourteen thousand miles of railway was owned by private companies. The governments of the various Australian states chartered private companies to build short lines out of the metropolis of each state. Railways were permitted to buy lands along their right of way at auction and in 1841, this price was fixed at £1 per acre. The government also supported private railway company ownership through loans, stock subscriptions, and guaranteed interest to investors. The Australians experimented with private ownership after 1904, but the experiment was largely a commercial failure (Clark, 1976).

In Japan, the initial development of railways from 1872 to 1904 was largely FPS funded. However, about 30 per cent of the railways were PPS owned (Hood, 2006: 18–20). Then, in 1904, almost all of the railway system was nationalised as a consequence of the Japanese-Russian war (Thuong, 1982). By 1910, the government ran 90 per cent of the railways (Hood, 2006: 20). There has been a combination of FPS and PPS funding support motivated by a combination of profit seeking and political prestige given to later twentieth-century developments of high-speed trains in Japan (Hood, 2006: 23).

Complementary Applications

Around the world, railways were applied to many uses in both freight and passenger services. Some of the most important applications that resulted, however, were spillovers that were external to the railroad itself but of profound, long-term importance to the economy as a whole. Rail was the key innovation at the core of a system of interrelated technologies that led to a new form of production and consumption. The managing of this time-sensitive, large-scale movement of products and inputs required a level of coordination whose precision was hitherto unknown. This was particularly so in the United States and Canada because of the huge distances involved. Telegraphic communications whose development in many cases preceded the development of railways, and were often financed by the PPS, were a critical complementary technology that permitted faster speeds for trains and in turn required more complex forms of organisation within the railway companies.[14] In an excellent

---

[14] See Du Boff (1980) and Reid (1886) for US examples.

example of technological complementarities, these new forms of organisation later spread to other industries.

> Of the new forms of transportation, the railroads were the most numerous, their activities the most complex, and their influence the most pervasive. They were the pioneers in the management of modern business enterprise . . . By the early twentieth century modern business enterprise, with its large staff of salaried managers and its clear separation of ownership and control, completely dominated the American transportation and communications networks – networks that were so necessary for the coming of mass production and mass distribution and for the rise of modern business enterprise in other sectors of the economy. (Chandler, 1977: 80)

Lessons

1. Many major new technologies often have large spillovers, as did the railroads. These cannot create profits for those who invest in the initial technology but give reason for considerable NPS support that may seem unprofitable on narrow financial calculations but is socially valuable, often massively so, when the spillovers are accounted for. The economic history of Canada, the United States, and Australia would have been vastly different if all finance for railroads had to come from the FPS, in which case there would have been no railroads for decades, if ever, and hence none of their vast externalities and broader spillovers.
2. Related to point 1, many major new technologies are developed by NPS support for non-economic reasons. For example, political and military motivations often drive NPS support for a technology which is later revealed to have generated great social and economic spillover benefits.

4.3.2 Automobiles

Under this heading, we include motor vehicles such as passenger cars, trucks, and busses. The automobile, like other transportation technologies, is actually a cluster of technologies related by complementarities. It integrates the many different technologies: the internal combustion engine, metals and plastics, a variety of machine tool and other mechanical devices, and, more recently, those of the information and communications revolution. Automobiles are an interesting case study for us in two ways. First, although there was little or no NPS support in any of this technology's trajectories in Europe and North America, there was major PPS support for creating the complementary infrastructure that allowed automobiles to flourish. Second, the Japanese and South

Korean post–World War II automobile industries are major triumphs of PPS support in the development trajectories for this technology.

Invention Trajectory

The invention trajectory of the automobile was exclusively financed by the FPS mainly because once the internal combustion engine was perfected, its applications to transportation vehicles were obvious and capable of producing profits over a fairly short time period. Most automobile companies were started by men who had previously manufactured bicycles or carriages. Indeed, the bicycle is one of the key technological antecedents to the motor vehicle and illustrates the value of having an existing and relevant facilitating structure. Components of bicycles that were incorporated into early automobiles included steel-tube framing, ball bearings, chain drive, and differential gearing. The bicycle industry's production technologies that were adopted by the motor vehicle industry include specialised machine tools, sheet metal, stamping, electric resistance welding, and the rubber tyre (Heitmann, 2009: 11–13). These early developments were FPS funded.

George B. Selden, Karl Benz, and Gottleib Daimler were key players in the invention and development of automobiles powered by internal combustion engines. All of their funding came from the FPS. Herbert Lee Barber lists more than one hundred manufacturers between 1899 and 1916 (Barber, 1917: 94–7), all of them FPS funded.

Efficiency and Applications-Diffusion Trajectories

As with the invention phase, commercial applications of the automobile were obvious once the requisite technology of the internal combustion engine was proven. As a result, again as with the invention phase, almost all the efficiency and applications-diffusion developments were FPS funded. There were, however, a few exceptions. For example, state support for some European motor companies began in a small way before 1914, with subsidies on various types of commercial vehicles which would be suitable for military purposes (Bloomfield, 1978: 105). There were also significant military procurement contracts in North America. Some early NPS funding was enjoyed by Henry Leland, who formed the Lincoln Motor Company in 1917. Leland and William Murphy, one of the initial financiers of Cadillac, arranged for $2 million in personal loans to start Lincoln, which began producing Liberty engines on a cost-plus basis for the military (Klepper, 2007: 112).

One of the most important ways in which the PPS supported the growth of the automobile industry (and the internal combustion engine) came in the form of road infrastructure in both Europe and North America (Barber, 1917: 166; Mackie & Smith, 2005: 216). During the 1930s, and again near the end of World War II, the US federal government funded highway development. The US Congress passed the Federal Aid Highway Act of 1944 (58 Stat. 838), which authorised construction of a system of multiple-lane, limited-access freeways. In 1956, the federal government agreed to provide 90 per cent of the initial construction expenses for these freeways and to raise the funds through tax increases on tyres, fuel, new vehicles, and a tonnage surcharge on trucks. To avoid diversion of automotive tax dollars into non-highway expenditures, the Highway Trust Fund was created. It was funded entirely by these taxes and used for roadway expenditures only. In general, most US highway projects continue to receive 80 per cent federal funding unless otherwise specified. Exceptions include interstate projects, which are 90 per cent funded, and some special projects that are fully funded (Rose & Mohl, 2012: 89).

Without this support by the governments in the United States and other countries, the motorised vehicle would not have had many of its most important applications – transporting goods and passengers commercially, reinforcing the growth of city suburbs that had begun with the suburban railway services, facilitating the growth of suburban shopping centres, and allowing the full development of the tourism industry.

The Japanese Post–World War II Automobile Industry

Following the import-substitution advice of economists such as Alexander Hamilton and Friedrich List, many countries used high tariff protection to create automobile assembly plants in the period between the two world wars. Most of these were infant industries that never really grew up sufficiently to survive even in local markets without tariff protection. So the conventional wisdom became that the protection of local automobile industries risked establishing only weaklings that could never stand up to international competition. This was widely believed on good evidence until the Japanese dramatically proved otherwise!

The Toyota Motor Company entered the automobile industry at the urging of the Japanese government shortly before World War II. After the war, Japanese automobile firms wanted to get into full-scale production in competition with the Europeans and Americans. Foreign producers were also anxious to start up in Japan.

Early on, the Japanese planning body, the Ministry of International Trade and Industry (MITI), made two key PPS interventions. It prohibited foreign firms from investing in the Japanese motor industry and it established high tariffs on imported cars. Without these initiatives, the Japanese industry would probably have become a branch plant industry using American technology, as did the Canadian industry. Instead, there was an influx of small, new local firms into the protected Japanese automobile industry.

In response to this influx, MITI attempted a third policy intervention, to rationalise the industry by turning the twelve existing Japanese firms into three big firms, each specialised in one branch of cars and trucks and with little competition among them. MITI's plan was based on the classic infant industry argument for tariffs, which was to allow the local infants to *move downwards along* a static, falling, long-run total cost curve and finally become as good as their foreign competitors. But in an industry characterised by technological change, competitors are a moving target. The experience of government-supported national flag carriers elsewhere suggests, however, that if MITI had had its way, the three specialised Japanese firms would have lacked the incentive to engage in the uncertain activity of major technological innovations while collecting the monopolistic rents created from a protected home market and thus would never have become major players internationally.

The Japanese auto firms resisted MITI's attempt to prevent what MITI regarded as 'excessive' competition and instead engaged in rivalrous competition. However, the Japanese market was not large enough to enable the firms to reach their minimum efficient scales (MESs) using American mass-production technology. What actually then happened illustrates the type of endogenous technological change that drives economic growth. After a lengthy process of trial and error, the firms invented the wholly new production technique of lean production, a critical component of which was just-in-time inventory management. Among other things, this enabled easier and earlier detection of design flaws, near elimination of inventories of parts, flexible and fast introduction, and switching of production among models and designs. In one of the great and not infrequent surprises in technological change, the MESs that were achieved at a lower-than-US volume of output were also at a lower unit cost than that achieved by the MESs of American plants.[15]

The key point is that the PPS had big impacts on the development of the automobile industry in Japan by inducing an FPS response. As is the case in many other technological developments, the NPS and the FPS worked together under conditions of uncertainty towards an outcome that neither sector fully anticipated or intended but one that ultimately, through lessons learned from both the successes and the mistakes experienced by both sectors, had great benefit.

---

[15] A full description can be found, for example, in Womack, Jones, and Roos (1990).

The Korean Post–World War II Automobile Industry

Korea's experience with the PPS-led development of their automobile industry was similar to Japan's in that the government played key roles in supporting the industry. However, the form of this support was quite different, being through export subsidies, import tariffs combined with collaboration and licensing agreements enabling access to the technologies of foreign firms (Lee & Mah, 2017). The PPS support targeted developing complementarities between manufacturers and parts suppliers within Korea so that scale and complementary component development could be co-developed.

The Automobile Industry Protection Act of 1962 began a policy process targeting the development of the automobile industry by restricting imports of foreign automobiles. But by 1967 and through the 1970s (with such policies as the Long-Term Automobile Promotion Plan of 1974), the policy was revised to target the industry with tax and subsidy incentives designed to support domestic and export production (Lee & Mah, 2017: 233).

In a process of learning by doing, policy was again refined in the 1980s with the Automobile Industry Rationalization Act of 1981 and the Automobile Industry Rationalization Act of 1987. Each of these policies was in response to how the industry was developing. Policy was redesigned to address oversupply and duplication of effort in a variety of activities within the industry (Lee & Mah, 2017: 234–5).

Enhanced transfer of technology to domestic small and medium-sized enterprises (SMEs) was a primary target of PPS support after 1993 with the Promotion Act for Collaboration of SME Automobile Parts Makers with Car Makers (KAMA, 2005: 446–8).

Technological transfers were also supported through PPS-funded education programmes and the building of domestic roadway infrastructure. These efforts targeted the development of the automobile industry from both the supply side in terms of skilled labour and the demand side in terms of infrastructure to support domestic demand for automobiles (Lee & Mah, 2017: 235–6).

Summary

Japan adopted the technology of automobile production proven elsewhere and altered it dramatically to fit the specific characteristics of its own manufacturing sectors using different forms of PPS support in cooperation (and sometimes conflict) with FPS actors. Korea did similar things in quite different ways. It also adapted many of the technologies it was utilising to its own specific manufacturing characteristics with a combination of PPS initiative and export-market orientation. The result in both cases was the development of context-specific (to each country's manufacturing sector characteristics), highly internationally competitive, automobile manufacturing industries. In the case of Japan, the creation of lean production was unforeseen by both the FPS and PPS agents involved in the original adoption of automobile production. Once created and proven within the Japanese automobile manufacturing industry, lean production in general and just-in-time inventory management conferred significant spill-over benefits in related technologies when adopted by manufacturing activities in many other lines of production.

Lessons

Original Development in the United States and Europe

1. Even when conditions are such that the FPS is motivated to finance all of the trajectories of a new technology, there may be room for NPS assistance when the full development of the technology requires much investment in infrastructure that is not suitable for FPS support.
2. Military procurement for efficiency trajectory can be important, even where it is not crucial, as was the case with motor vehicles (and aircraft).

Subsequent Followers in Japan and Korea

3. Governments sometimes can pick winners, as when MITI singled out the post-war automobile industry for encouragement. (We have relegated the broader question of the conditions under which governments are likely succeed or fail in picking winners to another paper (Lipsey & Carlaw, 2020).)
4. The uncertainty associated with PPS support of a technology new to one country can be greatly reduced if the FPS has already proven that the technology is workable elsewhere.
5. Pursuing a strategy of creating and supporting monopolistic national champions is not a likely route to policy success. Domestic competition is an important incentive, especially when innovation is required for continued success. Governments can err in trying to control the development of evolving firms by supressing such domestic competition, as MITI did when it tried to create three national champions who would not have been in competition with each other.
6. The international experience of successes and failures in establishing automobile industries in various countries illustrates the shortcomings in the traditional infant industry argument for tariffs that

is designed to assist a new industry in a developing country that is subject to substantial economies of scale when such industries are already established elsewhere. According to this argument, because capital markets are imperfect, the industry needs assistance to grow large enough to move to the bottom of an extended, negatively sloped, long-run cost curve (i.e., to fully exploit existing economies of scale). *Once the industry reaches efficient scale, the protection can be withdrawn* ... [However, since] technology is subject to continuous, endogenously generated change, effective infant industry protection cannot be seen as merely a matter of moving along a static long run cost curve. Instead, it is necessary to establish a dynamic industry that can hold its own in fierce international competition where technological change is one of the main weapons. (Lipsey, 2013: 43; italics added)

4.3.3 Aircraft

We use the term *aircraft* to cover an interrelated cluster of technologies. These have coevolved from a rudimentary understanding of lighter-than-air flight powered by a variety of primitive propulsion technologies, to sophisticated technologies that integrate complex, computer-assisted navigation and communication systems and are powered by advanced jet, rocket, and turbofan engines. The technology of aircraft integrates into complex transportation systems of delivery and departure nodes (themselves controlled by densely trafficked, electronic communications systems) of both civilian and military design. Aircraft have coevolved with several other major technologies of the nineteenth, twentieth, and twenty-first centuries (some of which are examined in the current Element), including communications, internal combustion engines, electricity, computers, materials, and organisation.

The coevolution of aircraft with many other complementary technologies illustrates what Nathan Rosenberg (1963) refers to as technological convergence. He observed convergence for aircraft in the use of technologies originally developed for bicycles being applied to the development of airframes. It is illustrated as well in the use of similar airframe technology being applied to two different power technologies of the internal combustion engine, first in piston form and later in jet form.

Invention Trajectory

In the cases of both the propeller and jet aircraft, the early invention of the technology was driven by private individuals who were possibly profit motivated, with the NPS (particularly the PPS) becoming heavily engaged in supporting the development of the efficiency and applications-diffusion trajectories once the technology had been proven.[16]

---

[16] It is not possible for us to determine if these private individuals were profit motivated or motivated by other things such as scientific and technological curiosity. We are convinced, however, that they were not supported by PPS or NGO institutional financing. This is why we have placed the technology of aircraft in Group 3.

Early precursors to the airplane were hot-air balloons, zeppelins, and fixed-wing gliders. Hot-air balloons appear to have originated in China in 220–208 BC, and they were PPS supported, used primarily for NEO, military signaling (Deng, 2005). Applications of the technology were supported by European PPS monarchs such as John V of Portugal and King Louise XVI of France, primarily for NEO, military applications once the technology was proven.

Zeppelins are lighter-than-air craft, the development of which was pioneered by their namesake, Count Ferdinand von Zeppelin (Chisholm, 1922). The basic design was a ridged frame that contained several gasbags similar in characteristic to hot-air balloons but filled with a lighter-than-air gas (de Syon, 2001). Zeppelin unsuccessfully sought NPS support from the German government for his design. Instead, FPS support for the design and building of the original zeppelins came from the Union of German Engineers and some German industrialists seeking profit (Dooley, 2004). Later, NPS support for the building of zeppelins came from both German and US military sources.

Fixed-wing gliders appear to have been based on such scientific principles as lift and drag. They appear to have been used mainly for sport by individuals who were not motivated by profit and therefore were in our NPS category (Harwood & Fogel, 2012). No clear PPS funding source is identifiable until well after such aircraft had been developed and proven. Once proven, these PPS funding sources were NEO, military applications.

The first pioneer of modern aeronautics was George Cayley in England. Between 1800 and his death in 1858, Cayley made many theoretical discoveries necessary for the invention of powered flight, including the importance of distinguishing among forces of weight, lift, thrust, and drag and overcoming challenges related to each. He also set out the conceptual design for a fixed-wing aeroplane requiring separate systems for lift, propulsion, and control. He was the first to successfully test stable fixed-wing gliding flight using first a four-foot model and later full-sized, manned gliders. Because he died before the invention of lightweight internal combustion engines, he was never able to achieve powered flight. His discoveries received no public or private funding and he appears to have been motivated by curiosity rather than profit and therefore is in our NPS class (Hallion, 2003: 110–14).

Further important theoretical and experimental discoveries, including the importance of a high wing-aspect ratio and the invention of the wind tunnel, were made after 1866 by NPS individuals in the member-funded Aeronautical Society of Great Britain (Hallion, 2003: 117). In France, Alphonse Penaud achieved the first successful heavier-than-air powered flight in 1871 using propellers wound with heavy cords – Penaud and Paul Gauchot created a larger, more sophisticated design, but it had technical deficiencies and lacked the power needed for flight (Hallion, 2003: 125). Penaud received no public or private funding and died penniless. Also in France, Victor Tatin successfully tested a compressed-air-driven seven-foot model which he funded himself (Hallion, 2003: 126). Another pre–Wright Brothers aviation pioneer in France was Clement Ader, who built the first steam-powered airplane, *Eole*, though there is no clear evidence that it successfully flew. Ader funded the development himself, and the trials were promising enough to secure military funding for development of the larger *Avion III-Aquilon*. Trials for this plane also failed for a variety of technical reasons. In the end, Ader spent an estimated $5 million (in 2001 dollars) in personal and public funds on the project (Hallion, 2003: 135). In England, the firearm designer Hiram Maxim spent $2 million of his own fortune building a testing machine powered by two 180 horsepower steam engines, though only once, in 1894, did it become airborne for a brief moment (Hallion, 2003: 143). Another pre–Wright Brothers pioneer was Samuel Langley, who successfully tested a thirteen-foot model powered by a 1 horse-power steam engine which flew thirty-three hundred feet in 1896. After this test, Langley was given $1 million (in 2001 dollars) by the US military to develop a full-sized version, the first ever military grant for research into heavier-than-air flight (Hallion, 2003: 150). Langley also received funding from Alexander Graham Bell and the Smithsonian (Hallion, 2003: 152). Both the PPS and FPS sources of funding proved insufficient since tests of the piloted craft in 1903 failed due to severe technical deficiencies.

We classify the invention chronology of the airplane to this point as belonging mainly to the NPS. This is not because it was mainly publicly funded but because much of the motivation for the private financing appears to be out of curiosity and therefore belongs in the NGO category of NPS. Where individual motivation appeared to be profit motivated, it sought support from publicly funded sources such as the military, both in terms of sales to these organisations and grants from them. So, where they were successful in these endeavors, they were NPS financed.

After many false starts, the airplane can be said to have been invented when in 1903, Wilbur and Orville Wright made the first powered flight in their airplane, *The Flyer*. Although they went on to profit from their invention and its patents, it does not appear that they invented the airplane for economic returns but rather were initially motivated by curiosity. Their invention therefore fits into our NGO category. They later sought profit from their invention in 1905, when they wrote to Secretary of War William Howard Taft offering to sell aircraft to the US government. They were definitely seeking profit throughout a series of patent litigations leading up to US government-mandated creation of a patent pool in 1917 (McFarland, 1953).

Efficiency and Applications-Diffusion Trajectories

These trajectories are so intertwined that it is not worth trying to deal with them separately. Once the Wrights flew, a mix of FPS, NGO, and PPS support began. One of the first instances of NEO funding for aircraft was in 1907, when the US Army Signal Corps signed a contract with the Wrights for the sale of one aircraft for $25,000 (approximately $748,550 in 2022 equivalent dollars) (Simonson, 1960). In the following years, other companies and individuals entered the market, including the Wright Company and the Curtiss Motor Company. Even with World War I approaching, growth in the industry was slow and the American '[f]ederal government's demand increased only gradually with the recognition of the potential of a military air arm' (Simonson, 1960).

During this period, several efficiency gains were made, particularly with respect to flight control (banking and rolling) using wing warping and aileron technologies. A patent for ailerons had been taken out in Britain in 1868 by Matthew Boulton, but this patent was all but forgotten by the time powered, manned flight took place (Magoun & Hodgins, 1931: 308). Early in the twentieth century, the Wright Brothers obtained various patents for flight control technologies, including those of wing warping and ailerons. A major NPS contribution to the early efficiency development of aircraft was an intervention of the US government prior to the outbreak of World War I in the form of mandated patent pooling which ended an ongoing litigation among various patent holders, including the Wright Brothers (McFarland, 1953: 23).

With the sudden large military demand during World War I, NPS funding quickly became (and remained) significant in the development of both the efficiency and applications-diffusion trajectories. The United States formed the National Advisory Committee for Aeronautics (NACA) in 1915 to 'undertake research basic to all aspects of aviation and flight', to further the science and technology of aeronautics, and to advise the military on purchases (Lawrence & Thornton, 2005: 9). The motivation for the PPS support was partially prestige, partially national defence, and partially long-term social returns due to anticipated spillovers. A large portion of the PPS support for aircraft in the United States was motivated by direct NEO, military demand and not because of perceived economic benefits (Brooks, 1967).

World War I also triggered tremendous growth in the industry in all of the belligerent countries, driven almost exclusively by PPS funding. Russia purchased several French-made aircraft. The Austro-Hungarian Empire invested in a series of technical failures labelled the 'Knoller Programme'. The British, French, and Americans all had their own construction and procurement processes which resulted in a post-war surplus of aeroplanes (Grosz, Haddow & Schiemer, 1993) By 1917, US appropriations for military aviation rose to $22,500,000 (Simonson, 1960). In 1917, Boeing received an order worth $600,000 from the US Navy for fifty Model C aircraft (Spitzer, 2004). The government also initiated a trade association, the Manufacturers Aircraft Association, in which rivals pooled patents and shared plane-making methods (Lawrence & Thornton, 2005: 9).

In the United States, the Air Mail Act of 1925 awarded contracts to private concerns for mail delivery (Lawrence & Thornton, 2005: 11). Although these were commercial contracts, they were awarded on favourable terms to encourage the private carriers. The Air Commerce Act of 1926 'charged the Secretary of Commerce with the responsibility for fostering air commerce through the establishment of airports, civil airways, and navigational aids' (Simonson, 1960: 365–6). It was a precursor to the Civil Aeronautics Act of 1938. This act created the Civil Aeronautics Authority, later called the Civil Aeronautics Board (CAB), to centralise the commercial and safety regulation of civil air travel. In addition to the five-member 'Authority', the act created a civil aeronautics administrator and a three-member Air Safety Board, all appointed by the president subject to the advice and consent of the US Senate. Key provisions of the act concerned regulations covering the registration and safety of air travel (3rd Session of the 75th US Congress, 1938: 973–1030).

The US federal government also provided PPS funding through the NACA from 1920 to 1930 by contributing to the design of several critical advances such as variable-pitch propellers, retractable landing gears, and fully cowled radial engines, as well as building wind tunnels, which led to further technological advancements in aircraft design (Lawrence & Thornton, 2005: 11). The PPS supported Lockheed and Northrop's design of cantilever monoplanes in the late 1920s. These evolved in the 1930s into the Boeing and Douglas all-metal, twin-engine cantilever monoplanes.[17] In 1929, Boeing began designing the B-9, which resulted from a US Army contract. The B-9 was converted into the Boeing 247, which is considered the world's first modern airliner. The 1930s also showed considerable PPS-supported development in air transport when the PPS supported the development of the Douglas DC-1, DC-2, and DC-3, which

---

[17] Advancements in technology in the 1920s enabled Charles Lindbergh to fly from New York to Paris in 1927, which spurred an 'explosion of public interest and investment in aviation projects and the firms undertaking them' (Lawrence & Thornton, 2005: 12).

directly competed with the Boeing 247.[18] In this period, the association, along with its clients in the Army Air Corps, lobbied successfully for continued government support for the industry through public operation of the air mail system and public funding of airports, flight control, and weather services (Markusen, 2000: 130).

US government support continued throughout World War II and thereafter. Indeed, support for research funding in the US commercial jet aircraft industry has been consistently high throughout its history. Between the 1930s and the 1990s, the US government regularly funded more than 75 per cent of R&D in the American aircraft industry, most notably during the 1950s and 1960s, when nearly 80 per cent of industry sales were to the government (Kenworthy, 1995: 106). Large commercial aircraft innovations in the United States have been supported primarily by the federal bodies of the NACA, NASA, US Department of Defense (DoD), and Federal Aviation Administration (FAA), all of which have provided long-term and stable research funding to the industry (Golich & Pinelli, 1997: 45). In 1989, the aerospace industry received from the federal government 82 per cent of all the funds it spent on R&D. This was 54 per cent of all federal funds spent on private-sector manufacturing R&D. Government patronage increased the industry's share of manufacturing output over the post–World War II period and particularly in the late 1970s, as increased world market integration and heightened competitive pressures set in (Markusen, 2000: 131). As of the turn of the twenty-first century, approximately two-thirds of the output of the aerospace industry was bought by the federal government (Wensveen, 2007: 4). This figure had risen as high as 74 per cent during the 1980s and 1990s (Wensveen, 2007: 4). At the same time, commercial applications proliferated.

European Developments

There has also been significant PPS support for the commercial aircraft industry throughout Europe and other parts of the world (Caliskan, 2010). In the mid 1920s, the developments in Europe, mainly Britain, France, and Germany, were heavily influenced by the PPS. Each country had several small FPS-funded airlines as early as 1919. These small pioneer companies, and others formed subsequently, were progressively amalgamated and nationalised during the 1920s until they formed national flag carriers. In 1924, Imperial Airways was formed in Britain with an annual £1 million subsidy guarantee to be maintained for ten years (Quin-Harkin, 1954). In 1926, Deutsche Lufthansa (later

---

[18] These developments were for early jet aircraft, which we discuss in more detail in the next section.

Lufthansa) was formed in Germany. This airline was fully PPS funded by the German government. In 1933, Air France was established and heavily PPS funded through to the end of World War II. Again, this was an amalgamation of several pre-existing airline companies which were themselves heavily PPS subsidised (Glab, 2003). In the early 1920s, most other European countries also formed their own nationalised airlines from pre-existing FPS firms engaged variously in the manufacture of aircraft and flying for commercial and public-sector purposes, all of which were PPS funded to some degree (Brooks, 1967).

Many early European jet aircraft manufacturing developments were PPS supported. One was the British Comet. It was initially developed by an initiative from the Cabinet of the United Kingdom's Brabazon Committee and the British manufacturer deHaviland for the national airline British Overseas Airways Corporation (BOAC). Another was the French Caravelle, developed out of an initiative from the PPS Comité du matériel civil (Civil Aircraft Committee) by a national manufacturer, the Société nationale des constructions aéronautiques du Sud-Est (SNCASE) (Mansfield, 1966; Todd & Simpson, 1986; Trischler & Zeilinger, 2003). The Comet was the first commercial jet-powered aircraft, but it suffered from technical design flaws that resulted in several fatal crashes and its ultimate failure in the commercial jet aircraft industry (Trischler & Zeilinger, 2003). Following on the heels of the Comet's failure and with many of the Comet's original design features (such as the cockpit configuration), the French Caravelle emerged as a leader in terms of technology and commercial applications to short- and medium-haul air travel (Mansfield, 1966; Todd & Simpson, 1986). In 1960, the Caravelle was the only short- and medium-haul jet aircraft in production and it outperformed its closest turbo prop competitors, the British Viscount and the US Convaire. However, later in that decade, much of the ongoing French R&D in jet aircraft design and manufacture was diverted into the more prestigious Concorde project. As a result, Caravelle lost its competitive edge to MacDonald Douglas and Boeing (Lipsey & Carlaw, 1996: 272).

The PPS-supported Anglo-French Concorde project was initiated in 1965 with the formation of the UK government's Supersonic Transport Committee, which recommended in 1959 the beginning of design work on supersonic airliners. In 1962, the Supersonic Aircraft Agreement between France and Great Britain was based on a commissioned report from the newly formed British Aircraft Corporation (BAC). The programme was a policy failure in economic terms. Cost overruns occurred in both the development stage of the technology and in the aircraft's operations. Large amounts of R&D funds were devoted to an unsuccessful attempt to overcome the sonic boom and the operating costs proved so high that airlines outside of France and the UK were unwilling to use it even if gifted to them. One significant side effect of the Concorde effort was that much was learned from it as an institutional and governance-building exercise. This benefited subsequent inter-country cooperative ventures, including the Airbus (Lipsey & Carlaw, 1996, 271). By far the most important PPS initiative in Europe was the Airbus, a manufacturing enterprise that was almost completely PPS supported in its initial development (Mowery, 1991: 90). While the Airbus may not have been judged a 'commercial success' in terms of recouping its initial development costs, Mowery emphasises that economic criteria are not the sole evaluative factor as '[m]uch of the motivation for the Airbus venture stems from the desire of European governments to maintain, for reasons of national security and economic development, a national aircraft design and production capability' (Mowery, 1991: 92).[19] Later versions of the Airbus have proven more successful commercially. Also, without Airbus, Boeing would probably have developed a monopoly on the design and production of long-range civilian transport aircraft. Instead, a duopoly developed with international competition 'reflected in continuous improvements in the quality of the aircraft, such as greater comfort, reduced fuel consumption and lower levels of pollutant emissions and noise' (Caliskan, 2010). Throughout their lifetimes, both companies have enjoyed significant PPS support in various forms.

Other significant PPS and NGO support has been received by the aircraft industry through support of complementary technologies such as the building of airports and other parts of the air transportation network. In the United States, almost all airports up to 1997 were publicly owned and operated by local city and regional authorities. In 1997, the US Congress established the FAA's Airport Privatization Pilot Program following the 1996 Reauthorization Act (Federal Aviation Administration, 2012). The Airport Privatization Pilot Program was established to test the case for private ownership of airports in the United States and had a small uptake (Federal Aviation Administration, 2012). Prior to 1987, British airports were virtually all 'publicly owned by a local, regional, or national government, by a semiautonomous public authority, or by some combination of these' (Bowen, 2010: 242). In 1986, Parliament passed the Airports Act, which moved to 'privatize the country's major airports, removing them from the state's balance sheet and opening them to a restricted form of private ownership' (McNeill, 2010).

---

[19] In the twenty-first century, Airbus is enjoying commercial success and is an established, internationally competitive rival to other airframe manufacturers.

4.3.4 Jet Engines

Invention Trajectory

Practical jet propulsion began soon after the invention of gunpowder, which was used to power rockets, first for fireworks then for military uses. The trajectory, driven by NPS, academic, and innovative curiosity, around the use of gunpowder as a propulsion fuel dates at least as far back as the seventeenth century (Dee, 2007). This fuel source was inefficient, however, so the next step, taken early in the twentieth century, was to use external power to compress air, which was mixed with fuel to provide thrust. Such engines never reached a level of efficiency to allow them to compete with conventional propellers on aircraft. Next came the gas turbine, or turbojet, which used the engine's own power to drive the compressor. This was the crucial breakthrough. It was originally patented in the late eighteenth century and used experimentally in the early twentieth. Then, in 1921, Maxima Guillaumme patented the first jet engine designed – but never employed – to propel an airplane. Starting in 1928, Frank Whittle, then a cadet at a Royal Air Force (RAF) training college, began work on a jet engine which he improved over the 1930s. The UK government showed little interest in Whittle's engine and he continued his work using his own resources. Whittle published much of his work and, while he did secure PPS and FPS financing for some of its development, it appears that most of his own motivation was out of pure curiosity (i.e., best placed in our NPS\NGO category). Eventually, well into the jet engine's efficiency and applications-diffusion trajectories, the UK government did realise the potential of the jet and used Whittle's engine to power the Gloster Meteor, a successful fighter that first saw action early in 1945. Once again there was a mix of NPS and FPS cooperation in the development of the technology (Scott, 1995).

In Germany, Hans von Ohain began work on another version of the turbojet in the mid 1930s. The German aircraft manufacturer Ernst Heinkel saw the promise in Ohain's engine and provided FPS financing for its further development, after which it was used to power the Heinkel He 178, the first jet-powered airplane to take to the air (Scott, 1995). It appears that this was a solely FPS-funded venture.

Efficiency

The turbojet engine was further improved in performances with PPS support during World War II. The German aircraft firm Junkers developed a much-improved jet engine that was used for military purposes in the Me 262, which came into operation in mid 1944 and was highly successful, being credited with more than fifty kills of Allied aircraft.

In the post–World War II period in the United States, the NACA concentrated its research efforts on improving aircraft speed using the newly developed turbojet and rocket engines (Conway, 2005: 6). By this time, however, Britain had jumped into the lead using PPS support. DeHavilland was supported by the British Ministry of Supply, which guaranteed an order of fourteen Comets to the BOAC. This was done at the same time that the leading American commercial aircraft manufacturers, Douglas and Lockheed, were mandated by the government-regulated airline industry to focus on improving conventional propeller plane technology (Schnaars, 1994: 69).

The transformation of the aircraft industry during the early 1950s with the production of the jet-powered airplane was largely supported by PPS in Britain, the United States, and France. The disastrous failure of the British Comet led to an understanding of the stresses encountered when flying at high speed in high altitudes. It also illustrates that being first mover is not always advantageous when revolutionary new technologies are being developed. PPS support in Europe and the United States catalysed many other industry-wide changes, including new types of engines, airframes, on-board equipment, tooling and facilities, and, most important, a higher degree of complexity in products and the methods used to produce them. The highly successful PPS/ NEO-funded Boeing 707 was originally built as a military transport. It and the Douglas DC-8 instituted a new era in US aeronautical dominance, which saw the 'entire commercial engine market … become a jet-engine market' (Mowery, 1998: 66). It was the 'dual development of a civil and defense product [that] was critical to Boeing's commercial success' (Lawrence & Thornton, 2005: 40). The Boeing 747 was another significant aircraft that was heavily PPS/NOE supported, particularly in the development of its powerful jet engines.

Applications-Diffusion

The vast majority of planes that take to the air today are jet powered, as are many military missiles. Modified versions of the jet engine are also used for many other purposes such as industrial and commercial gas turbines, usually for stationary electricity generation, marine power plants, and modes of propulsion for other transportation technologies such as ships, automobiles, locomotives, and drones. These applications have been developed by the FPS for the most part. Where there was NPS support for jet engine applications it was mainly from military procurement in many countries.

As well as the significant direct support, much of the economic impact of NPS actions with respect to aircraft has been indirect, operating through the creation of opportunities in other, complementary technologies. These include airports, other transportation networks, and myriad other technologies linked to transportation systems, including, for example, refrigeration for the transportation of perishable goods.

Lessons

1. NPS/FPS cooperation in technological activities is important for success in many technological developments that have long investment trajectories full of uncertainties.
2. The uncertainty associated with PPS support of a new technology can be greatly reduced if the FPS has already proven that the technology is workable while there is a long future to its efficiency and applications trajectories, some of which developments are in the nature of spillovers whose value cannot be appropriated by the original developers.
3. Where there are close substitutes to some new technology, NPS agents are often reluctant to accept the risks associated with developing it until some FPS agent demonstrates its viability.
4. Being first mover in developing some radically new technology is not always advantageous, as illustrated by the disastrous failure of the British Comet.

4.3.5 Agriculture

In the case of agriculture, it is difficult to separate our trajectories since the invention of new strains can be regarded either as a new invention or an improvement in the efficiency of some generic crop. For that and for several other related reasons, we do not separate these trajectories but concentrate on the source of the funding of new technologies, of improvements in existing ones, and of new applications and diffusion.

General Support

Innovations and developments in agriculture have been supported by the NPS for millennia. An example is found in the hydrological developments in Sumer around 3000 BC, where vast irrigation works were created to produce crops that greatly increased agricultural surpluses. These were entirely PPS funded via a newly created tax-and-transfer system enabled by the invention of the GPT of writing, which had (and continues to have) the massive positive socio-economic spillovers described by Dudley (1991). These PPS-supported initiatives enabled the development of large cities that exhibited a high degree of specialisation of urban economic activities supported by agricultural surpluses. Unfortunately, technological change always occurs under conditions of uncertainty and no one foresaw the soil salination large-scale irrigation typically creates. Some five hundred years after irrigation began, salination led to the collapse of the sophisticated Sumerian society the technology had helped to build (Dudley, 1991; Thompson, 2004; Wright, 2004). But the world still had writing!

More recently (from the late nineteenth century to date), there has been significant NGO and PPS support for agricultural research coming from a variety of sources in Canada, the United States, Japan, Australia, New Zealand, and parts of Europe, Africa, and South America. The following are selected examples illustrating the extensive support by NGOs and the PPS in a variety of agricultural technology developments.

- In 1874, at the request of Dutch tea planters, the Dutch government recommended changes to the planting strategy which improved crop productivity (Maat, 2011: 189).
- In 1893, wheat breeding was started at the Japanese National Agricultural Experimental Station. By 1995, there were five national and two prefectural agricultural experimental stations that between them had registered 143 new varieties (Hoshino & Seko, 1996).
- In 1899, the US Department of Agriculture engaged in rice and crop field experiments (Maat, 2011: 189).
- In 1907, Pima cotton was developed by the US Bureau of Plant Industry (Rice, 1978: 140).
- Between 1960 and 1969, the International Rice Research Institute (IRRI) in the Philippines developed a dwarf semi-tropical rice named IR8 (Peng & Kush, 2003: 158).
- In 1962, a research collaboration between Mexico and Canada succeeded in developing two semi-dwarf wheat varieties, and another robust variety in 1996 (Reynolds & Borlaug, 2006: 6).
- Between 1968 and 1994, the Food and Agricultural Administration of the United Nations ran 'farmer field schools' in developing countries on integrated pest management (Zadoks, 2003: 187).
- Several agricultural research institutes have been directly supported by the PPS. These include the US Land Grant Colleges that began in 1862, the Pima Research Station in 1907, the UK's Rowett Research Institute in 1922, and the Netherlands' Agricultural College (Rice, 1978: 140).
- Several international NPS-supported institutions are directly involved in agricultural research. One is the Consultative Group on International Agricultural Research, formed in 1971 and organised by the World Bank and the United

Nations Development Programme (Ruttan, 2001: 215). Another is the IRRI, founded in 1960 as a joint effort between the University of Philippines, the Ford Foundation, and the Rockefeller Foundation, which was a key element of the Green Revolution discussed next (Fletcher, 2012: 21).

The Green Revolution

The Green Revolution, which occurred between the 1950s and the 1970s, was produced by research concerning agricultural technologies. It was largely initiated and conducted by developed economies with the purposes of developing new technologies and transferring technology and production know-how to developing economies (Hazell, 2009; Tribe, 1994).

The revolution was started with funding from the Rockefeller Foundation but soon obtained funding from several PPS and other NGO sources. Between the 1940s and the late 1970s, it increased agriculture production worldwide. Among the innovations were the development of irrigation infrastructure, high-yielding and disease-resistant varieties of cereal grains, and the application of hybridised seeds, synthetic fertilisers, and pesticides. These greatly increased crop yields for many of the developing economies where they were implemented.

One of the NPS contributions to the Green Revolution occurred in the form of research institutions that focussed mainly on cereals, rice, cotton, and sugar cane production, creating new robust varieties that could successfully grow in what were originally difficult environments. Some NPS support went to dairy and cattle production while a limited amount went to pesticide development. However, in the case of the latter two, most of the development occurred because of FPS support. Almost no NPS support went into the development of efficiency and applications for agricultural machinery.

One hugely positive but unintended impact of the Green Revolution has been on the development of the GPT of biotechnology. The FPS has largely led the research into agricultural applications of biotechnologies because of the many opportunities NPS-supported research has opened in this area. 'Agricultural biochemistry now found in biotechnology a common technical basis with breeding' (Buttel, Kenney & Kloppenburg, 1985: 37). Companies such as Monsanto, Agrigenetics, Calgen, Chevron, Pfizer, ARCO, Advanced Genetics Research, Zoecon Corporation, and the DNA Plant Technology Company have invested massively in biotechnology applications in agricultural technologies (Buttel et al., 1985: 35–7). The key point here is that the NPS-led Green Revolution created tremendous opportunities the FPS then exploited in an ongoing research programme that integrates agricultural technologies with biotechnology.

The NPS-supported research of the Green Revolution has also produced some unfortunate and unintended side effects along with its positive benefits. The huge and increasing reliance on pesticides and petrochemical-based fertilisers, which were critical to the new methods developed by Green Revolution research, contributed greatly to increases in greenhouse gas emissions and other pollutants, soil salination, and crop homogenisation. Pesticides are also currently having a devastating impact on bees, a critical natural polliniser (Fitzgerald-Moore & Parai, 1996; Hazell, 2009).

Lessons

1. In many fields, including agriculture, successful new products and new production processes would never have been undertaken by the FPS. This was both because they were public goods that could not be appropriated by individual agents in the FPS, and because they required very long gestation periods characterised by significant uncertainty before becoming productive.
2. The role NPS had in developing agricultural technologies, which have generated massive spillovers and profit for FPS agents who exploited the original inventions, demonstrates the broader positive impact NPS intervention can have when implemented in a timely fashion and in cooperation with FPS actions.
3. Because of uncertainty, the final benefits of any NPS (or FPS) initiative may be less than anticipated at the outset because of unforeseen private and social costs, or they may be more than anticipated because of unexpected spillovers.

4.4 GROUP 4: NPS Mainly in Invention and Efficiency Trajectories

4.4.1 Iron Steamship

The iron steamship was born out of the confluence of long development trajectories of sail-powered ships, metal technologies, and mechanical power (particularly steam) in the later eighteenth and nineteenth centuries.[20] Although not widely regarded as a GPT on its own, it was a technology that produced great social and economic transformations.

Invention Trajectory

As with many other technologies that developed over long periods of time, it is hard to say when the invention trajectory of the iron steamship ended and the

---

[20] The three-masted sailing ship with square sails on the two forward masts and a lateen sail on the aft mast enabled voyages of discovery and elevated globalized trade to historically unprecedented levels from the fifteenth century to the nineteenth century.

efficiency and applications-diffusion trajectories began. The invention trajectory had three strands: the steam engine, screw propulsion, and the use of iron. We take the invention trajectory to end when fully iron-hulled steamships driven by screw propellers came into use.

Once high-pressure engines had been developed in the early years of the nineteenth century, steam engines had their first marine use beginning in river vessels and harbour tugs. Boiler explosions with the new high-pressure engines were frequent. Once this technology had been mastered, steam engines were used for larger ocean-going ships. These ships were of wooden construction with paddle wheels providing the motive power. The first Atlantic crossing that used steam, at least in part, was in 1819 by the US ship the SS *Savannah*, a hybrid of wooden construction equipped with sail but with a steam engine for use in calm weather (Morison, 1903). The first ship powered solely by steam, the *Aaron Manby*, crossed the English Channel in 1822. The first Atlantic crossings under steam alone occurred around 1830. The ship was the *Great Western*. It was an oak-hulled, ironclad, hybrid sail-steam vessel built expressly for Atlantic crossing, although still driven by paddle wheels (Corlett, 1975). The *Savannah*, the *Aaron Manby*, and the *Great Western* were all FPS financed.

There was initial resistance, particularly from the Royal Navy, to the use of iron for hulls but wood supply shortages and other market factors drove the British to find innovative solutions. Iron was proved in 1839 when a storm drove an iron steamer (the *Garry Owen*) ashore along with several wooden boats. All the wooden boats were destroyed while the *Garry Owen* was undamaged (Thiesen, 2006).

In 1835, two inventors in Britain, first Francis Pettit Smith and then John Erikson some weeks later, patented the first practical screw propellers (Bourne, 1852). Experiments on models and small ships proved that the screw worked but the British Admiralty was sceptical, maintaining it would be impractical in heavy weather. That view was soon challenged by observing a screw-driven ship preforming well in heavy weather. The Admiralty then encouraged Smith to build a full-sized ship to further test that means of propulsion (Bourne, 1852). This ship, the wooden-hulled *Archimedes*, was built in 1838 by the private shipbuilder Henry Wimshurst with FPS funding (Herapath, 1839). Isambard Kingdom Brunel enjoyed PPS support by helping the Admiralty with testing of screw propulsion on the *Archimedes*. Erikson built a screw-driven, steam-powered,/sailing ship, the *Robert F. Stockton*, in 1839, which he sailed to the United States, where it attracted the attention of the US Navy. Erikson became the designer of the US Navy's first screw-driven ship, the USS *Princeton* (Bourne, 1852). This shift from paddle wheels to the screw propeller required several important inventions to allow a reciprocating steam engine to provide a direct drive to a fore-and-aft shaft connected to an external propeller. In 1840, the *Archimedes* took part in trials against paddle wheel–driven ships and proved successful. Subsequent voyages created great interest in this method of propulsion. As a result of its success, the Royal Navy adopted screw propulsion (Thiesen, 2006).

In 1840, the *Archimedes* accomplished the first regularly scheduled Atlantic crossing. Then, in 1847, the success of the *Archimedes* led Brunel to adopt screw propulsion on his new solely FPS-financed ship, the *Great Britain*, which became the first iron-hulled, propeller-driven ship to cross the Atlantic. The age of the iron steamship had arrived.

> The services which Mr. Brunel rendered to the country during the whole of these proceedings were given entirely without pecuniary recompense, and in the face of opposition and discouragement; but he had the satisfaction of knowing that he had been mainly instrumental, not only in introducing the screw propeller into the mercantile navy, but also in securing its adoption in Her Majesty's fleet. (Brunel, 1870: 288)

In the United States, the FPS pioneered the development of iron shipbuilding, primarily in the mid-Atlantic states. Beyond a few military contracts for iron ships in the United States, almost all of the activity appears to have been FPS funded.

Efficiency and Applications-Diffusion Trajectories

An early US PPS-supported application of iron steamships was the *City of Peking*, an iron-hulled, screw-driven, steam- and sail-powered passenger and freight ship build by the Pacific Mail Steamship Company with a $500,000 subsidy from the US Congress (Swann, 1965: 80). This is one example of several ships built in the United States and Britain with some form of PPS support to compete in transatlantic and Far East trade routes.

Other PPS support for the building and development of ships came soon after the navies in Britain and the United States converted to screw propulsion and iron hulls. This took the form of schools, professional societies, publication of theoretical works, and experimental research (Thiesen, 2006). The Royal Navy provided numerous postal subsidies and naval subventions that helped to finance the construction of passenger liners and freighters.

In 1860, naval architects and shipbuilders created the NPS Institution of Naval Architects whose membership included the people in the British Admiralty. The Institution raised money from its members, but it was so important to the Admiralty that whenever the Institution was unable to raise the necessary funds, the Admiralty would provide the balance (Thiesen, 2006). In 1864, the Admiralty and the Institution co-founded a British school of naval architecture which comprised professionals who mostly worked for the Royal Navy and Lloyd's Society (Thiesen, 2006). Most of the activities of the Institution were involved with the science of building iron ships. These activities enjoyed significant PPS support. In the second half of the nineteenth century, shipbuilding was aided by the emergence of naval architecture programmes in educational institutions, including Glasgow University in 1884, Armstrong College in 1890, and Liverpool University in 1908.

The enabling role NPS support provided in developing and refining the cluster of steam power, screw propellers, and iron hulls provided positive links to future technologies such as the internal combustion engine, which later substituted for steam but was itself complementary to screw propellers and iron and later steel hulls.

Lessons

1. As already observed with many developments in aircraft, the existence of close substitutes, this time in the form of sailing ships, made NPS agents reluctant to accept the uncertainties associated with the new technologies of iron hulls and screw propellers until FPS agents had proven their superiority.
2. The role of the NPS is often not motivated by economic concerns, even though what follows generates technological complementarities that when exploited generate spillovers. The early NPS support of iron steamships and screw propellers were for naval purposes in most cases.

4.5 GROUP 5: NPS Support for All Three Trajectories

4.5.1 Electricity

Electricity is our term for a collection of power-generating technologies that differ significantly from their predecessors of animate and inanimate power technologies in that electricity delivers kinetic energy as a flow of electrons. This enables an unprecedented flexibility in its generation and set of applications compared to any mechanical power technology currently known. Electricity is generated from a variety of technologies including batteries, in which electricity is generated through a chemical reaction; solar, which uses a photo-voltaic process to generate electric current; and hydro, gas, coal, tidal, and nuclear power generation. Our discussion focusses on batteries and the dynamo as key technologies in the historical development of electricity.

The Invention Trajectory[21]

The development of electricity as a power source provides a contrast to the other technologies reviewed in what follows, particularly the computer, the Internet, and the laser, in that its invention trajectory was almost exclusively financed by NPS support. In his great book *De Magnete*, William Gilbert (physician to the English Crown in the early seventeenth century and Fellow of the Royal College of Physicians, London), brought together all of the ad hoc knowledge about the behaviour of the compass needle that had been known for centuries to the Chinese and others with his unifying hypothesis that the earth is a giant loadstone whose magnetic North Pole is situated just below the earth's surface, near – but not at – the geographic North Pole. This turned a body of empirical observations on the behaviour of the compass needle into a genuine theory of magnetism (Pumfrey, 2002). In 1670, Otto von Guericke (a university-trained political figure) invented a machine to produce an electric charge. At the start of the eighteenth century, Du Fay (a member of the French Academy of Science) showed the difference between positive and negative electric charges. The earliest form of condenser, the Leyden jar, was independently invented in 1745 by Pieter van Musschenbroek, a Dutch mathematician and physicist, and Ewald Georg von Kleist, a German cleric, both of whom we classify in the NPS. In 1752, Benjamin Franklin (Fellow of the Royal Society) showed that atmospheric electricity was identical in form to the charge produced by a Leyden jar. In 1766, Joseph Priestley (Fellow of the Royal Society) proved that the force between electric charges varies inversely with the distance between the charges. Charles-Augustin de Coulomb (French military engineer and physicist) subsequently invented an instrument to measure electric charges accurately. All of these discoveries were motivated by an interest in pure science and financed by funds from NGO sources.

In 1800, Alessandro Volta (professor of physics) produced the first electric battery, the voltaic pile, which for the first time gave electricity obvious commercial applications. The invention trajectory of electricity then continued on to the dynamo while the battery entered its efficiency and applications-diffusion trajectories.

The Battery: Efficiency and Applications-Diffusion Trajectories

The early development of more efficient batteries received a great deal of NGO support. Those involved were often professors at European universities or

---

[21] We provide a selective list of the basic discoveries on the trajectory that led first to the battery and then to the dynamo.

university-trained scientists. Non-governmental organisations such as the Royal Institution of Great Britain[22] (which at one point housed Faraday's research laboratory) and the Royal Society[23] played key roles in communicating results to other scientists and financially supporting them. Volta enjoyed NGO funding in several forms. For example, he received the Royal Society's Copley Medal, which came with a sizeable financial prize. Within a year of Volta's letter to the Royal Society describing his pile, members of the Royal Society began experimenting on and building their own stronger batteries (Schlesinger, 2010: 48).

The Royal Institution of Great Britain funded experiments, hosted lecturers, and employed many scientists working on the development of electricity, most notably Humphry Davy and Michael Faraday. To overcome the deficiencies of the weak patent system of the day that made manufacturers reluctant to share their processes with the public, the Institution facilitated the sharing of knowledge by building one of the best-equipped labs in Europe and inviting key players to do research there (Schlesinger, 2010: 50). NGO support was also provided by the Royal Society, which supported many of the breakthrough inventions that occurred during the development of the battery. It also rewarded inventors with financial prizes.

The PPS funding for the development of the battery included Napoleon's commission to build a six-hundred-cell battery at the Ecole Polytechnique in Paris. The Royal Institution of Great Britain funded the building of a two-thousand-cell battery in 1808 (Atheron, 1984: 24–5; Schlesinger, 2010: 60). In 1809, Humphry Davy used the Royal Institution's two-thousand-cell battery to create an electric arc between two electrodes, an early experiment that led to the use of electricity as a source of lighting. These early NGO- and PPS-funded experiments led to several commercial applications focussed on the field of chemistry with experiments that isolated elements. Early batteries were also increasingly used in commercial electroplating.

In 1866, Georges Leclanché developed the first prototype of the battery most commonly used today, the 'dry cell' battery. He developed the prototype while working in the FPS as an engineer (Pire, 2018).

The widespread use of the telegraph required significant refinements to the battery. Although in the United States, Samuel Morse was a central figure in this development, he mainly drew together existing scientific knowledge developed

---

[22] The Royal Institution was founded by a group of scholars and scientists for philanthropic purposes. It was initially privately (but obviously NGO) funded but later enjoyed direct PPS funding.

[23] The Royal Society was founded under a charter of the king of England in 1662. In the seventeenth century, the Society was funded entirely by contributions from Fellows – although it was granted lands by the Crown in 1669, which were sold back to the Crown for £1,300 in 1682 (Bluhm, 1958). Only in 1849 was direct PPS funding provided, starting in that year at £1,000 - per year and increasing over successive decades (Hall, 1981).

through NGO-funded academic research in Europe and the United States. Morse also secured $30,000 in PPS funding from the US federal government to construct an experimental telegraph line from Baltimore to Washington, DC. This proved such lines were feasible and helped to overcome the resistance of private investors to risk funds in telegraph development. By 1850, there were twelve thousand miles of telegraph, much of which was financed by FPS firms. Nonetheless, in 1861, the US government subsidised the building of a transcontinental line which was completed in four months (Schlesinger, 2010: 111).

The development of the telegraph in Europe was similar to the experience in the United States. A private citizen, Fothergill Cooke, built an early telegraph machine using indirect NGO funding in the form of consultations with publicly funded academics such as Charles Wheatstone, a professor at Kings College in London, and Joseph Henry (Atherton, 1984). British railways eventually adopted Cooke's machine to use in their signalling. In 1870, the telegraph system in England became entirely PPS funded with the nationalisation of the entire system for £8 million (Atherton, 1984).

Electricity's Invention Trajectory Continued. The invention of the battery in 1800 was followed by a series of NPS- and FPS-financed discoveries in electricity. Faraday's work was disseminated through the Royal Society and provided the basis for many of the early devices. NGO institutions such as the Royal Society produced periodicals which communicated discoveries and disseminated information on early developments of electricity to the United States through the *American Journal of Science* (Gee, 1993).

In 1819, Hans Christian Oersted demonstrated that a magnetic field existed around an electric current. In 1831, while at the Royal Institution of Great Britain, Faraday demonstrated that a current flowing through a coil of wire could induce a current in a nearby coil; he also developed the theory of electric lines of force. In 1840, James Joule, a self-taught scientist, demonstrated that electricity was a form of energy and that it obeyed the law of the conservation of energy. Joule also showed that the magneto converts mechanical energy into electrical energy. It is difficult to say how much of his work was motived by scientific curiosity and how much by attempts to improve the efficiency of the brewery he managed. In 1845, Wheatstone and Cooke patented an electromagnet to replace a permanent magnet in telegraphs. Wheatstone was an NPS-supported academic, but both he and Cooke received funding from the FPS Birmingham Railway Company (Atherton, 1984). In 1866, the self-financed engineer Dr. Henry Wilde, apparently motivated by pure scientific curiosity and therefore in our NGO classification, described a machine that used an electromagnet to turn unlimited amounts of mechanical energy into electrical energy. In 1873, James Maxwell published his *Treatise on Electricity and*

Magnetism, which mathematised Faraday's theory of electrical magnetic forces. As he was a university-supported scientist, his was an NPS-financed activity.

Following Faraday's and Henry's early experiments with electromagnetism, Hippolyte Pixii constructed what is widely considered the first electric generator, a magneto (Atherton, 1984: 112). As the device was developed, the coil segment was improved and an electromagnet powered by a battery or other generating device was used. Although there is some uncertainty as to who developed the first dynamo, in 1867, Wheatstone, an academic, Ernst Siemens, an industrialist, and Simon Varley, an electrical engineer, independently invented practical dynamos. The electric engine had arrived with many of its by-then obvious commercial applications.

Electricity: Efficiency and Applications-Diffusion Trajectories

The transition from magneto to dynamo that was made after 1867 was almost entirely supported by the FPS. However, some of the initial adoptions and adaptations of the dynamo in and around 1867 were made by people such as Dr. Wilde, a man of private wealth who experimented in electrical engineering and was among the first to replace permanent magnets with electromagnets. It appears that his experiments and research were self-funded. He wrote of his results to Faraday, who communicated them broadly to and through the Royal Society (Atherton, 1984: 122). It would seem that his motives were not profit.

The motivations of others place them clearly in the FPS. While Siemens and Wheatstone are credited with inventing the first practical dynamo, Zenobe T. Gramme, a carpenter who became involved in electrical experiments, made an adjustment to the magneto in 1870 which allowed it to produce a constant current, creating a commercially useful dynamo for the Alliance company. The Gramme dynamo was then manufactured and became the first dynamo sold commercially (McMahon, 1984: 20–1). It was initially used mainly in the electroplating industry. All of these activities were for profit.

In 1877, the Franklin Institute of Philadelphia held a competition for manufacturers of dynamos.[24] Three models competed – one from Charles Brush, one from Gramme, and one from William Wallace and Moses Farmer. Brush was a chemist based at the University of Michigan, so some of his work was indirectly NGO funded (McMahon, 1984: 21). Brush's machine won the Franklin Institute's competition for efficiency and design and he went on to form a company, similar to Thomas Edison's, that operated power stations and

---

[24] This NGO was initially funded by private money provided by Samuel Vaughan Merrick and William H. Keating. The former was a manufacturer and the latter was a geologist and university professor.

arc lamps in large cities. The development of the dynamo and lighting beyond this point appears to have been exclusively FPS funded as private financiers began investing in these companies that operated their own privately funded research labs.

The invention phase of electricity was mostly NPS supported while, with a few exceptions, the transition from the magneto to the dynamo and the movement into the efficiency and applications-diffusion phases was mostly FPS supported.

The electrical grid we have today could not have existed without alternating current (AC). Early work by NPS-funded scientists was taken up by private experimenters and entrepreneurs after the viability of the technology was proven. (This sequence is true for direct current (DC) as well.) For example, Nikola Tesla's patents and Westinghouse's FPS financing played a role in propelling AC technology to where it needed to be for large-scale generation and transmission projects (Schewe, 2007: 53–5).

Following breakthroughs in dynamo and lighting technologies, private companies began to provide electric lighting in local areas of large US cities (e.g., the Edison Company and the Brush electric company).[25] The first and most prominent facility was the Pearl Street distribution station built by Edison in Manhattan. The station ran on DC and therefore was limited to approximately two miles for transmission (Bedell & Pierce, 1928). Alternating current, which could use extremely high voltages to transmit over very long distances, eventually overcame this limitation.

The first major transmission project in the United States was part of the infrastructure to transmit power generated at Niagara Falls. It was entirely FPS financed (Schewe, 2007).

Rural Electrification

Rural electrification in the United States (and other countries) represented major PPS contributions to electricity's efficiency and applications-diffusion trajectories. Private companies were keen to earn expected profits from providing electricity to major urban and suburban areas, but profit incentives were lacking for rural electrification.

Rural electrification was accomplished almost exclusively through PPS support in the United States (and several other countries). Electrical power for the rural United States had been under consideration by public authorities

---

[25] Many of the early applications and demonstrations of the dynamo were in providing power for various forms of lighting. The development of the dynamo coincided with the development of electric light (Bedell & Pierce, 1928).

since the early 1900s as both a social issue and as an untapped market.[26] The low productivity and the high poverty of those living on US farms was a concern of politicians. However, FPS firms did not consider social welfare when looking at rural areas and profit margins were usually too low compared to urban areas to induce them to provide rural electrification on their own (Slattery, 1940: 6).

Before World War I, electrical co-ops were set up to overcome the high costs and provide power to rural residents at lower cost than power companies could provide. However, in many cases, the co-ops failed financially. Their service grids were then bought up by private companies that charged higher prices in segments that could support them and stopped service altogether in segments where profits could not be realised (Brown, 1980: 15).

World War I brought a boom in demand for agricultural output and a national security argument was tied to the social argument for rural electrifications (Saloutos, 1982: 3). In spite of increases in the power supply due to the construction of several hydroelectric dams by the US Army Corps of Engineers (USACE), supported by PPS funding after the war, there was little support for providing electricity to farms because of a perceived lack of demand on the part of farmers (Slattery, 1940: 11–14). The PPS advocates for rural electrification argued, however, that while farm electrification would not pay through direct farm use, there might be a bigger pay-off from the creation of new, small rural industries (Slattery, 1940: 4). This was a predicted social spillover driven by the complementary relations among farming, electricity production, and rural industries that had benefits well above private returns.

In 1923, the Committee on the Relation of Electricity to Agriculture (CREA) was created as a partnership between the private power industry (represented by the National Energy Lighting Association (NELA)), state agricultural colleges, and the American Farm Bureau Federation (Brown, 1980: 3). The objective of the CREA was to increase rural electrification, focussing on convincing farmers to use more electricity and not on convincing private industry to lower their price (Brown, 1980: 5). The CREA made little progress during the Great Depression and was considered a failure.

The Rural Electrification Administration (REA), which was created in 1935, embodied the 'Goal of Parity': rural electricity provided at reasonable rates and service comparable to urban areas (REA, 1966: 22). Rural electrification was included in the emergency relief projects and $100 million was approved in the

---

[26] In 1911, a report on electrical use in rural, non-irrigation areas was presented at the National Electric Light Association (NELA) convention in New York. This report encouraged electricity providers to consider the rural market but also argued that the market price needed to be the same as in urban areas (Slattery, 1940: 3).

Emergency Relief Appropriation Act in April 1935 (Slattery, 1940: 30). From 1935 to 1966, the REA increased the proportion of electrified farms from 11 per cent to 98 per cent.

> Perhaps one of the greatest contributions the New Deal made to agriculture was expanding the use of electricity on the farms. This, of course, was tied in to a very great extent with the achievements of the TVA [Tennessee Valley Authority]. Beginning in 1935 on a modest scale and outside the USDA [US Department of Agriculture], the REA expanded its activities in the years prior to the outbreak of World War II and especially after peace was restored. The federal government under the New Deal assumed a responsibility that the private utilities had been unwilling to assume and that they continued to resist until they saw the futility of their actions. And because of the spread of electricity in the rural areas under REA auspices, crop and livestock production improved: a wider use of farm machinery became possible; labor costs decreased; greater use was made of modern, efficient techniques of farming; much backbreaking toil and drudgery came to an end; the use of indoor plumbing and refrigeration spread; improved means of communication became possible; rural education benefited; and the morale of the farm wife was lifted. (Saloutos, 1982: 268)

The demand for electricity from farmers began at a low level as their capital equipment was not set up for electrification. But over the years, as new equipment was purchased, such as electric milking machines and refrigeration facilities for home and barn, demand rose dramatically. Finally, when all the long-term adjustments had been made, electricity provision became a paying proposition for the FPS.

Other countries were also successful in using PPS support to electrify their rural areas during the interwar period. Ontario, Canada, is often used as an early example of the successful provision of electricity to rural areas. In 1908, the Hydro-Electric Commission of Ontario was created as a public utility. It generated electricity, subsidised half the cost of distribution lines, and provided loans for electric appliances (Brown, 1980: 17). The Canadian federal government then subsidised rural power to help agriculture out of the recession (Slattery, 1940: 31). Governments provided considerable aid to rural electrification in several other countries. In Sweden, 50 per cent of farms were electrified by 1936 through NGO-co-ops. In both Germany and France, 71 per cent of farms gained access to electricity through government support (Brown, 1980: 16).

Summary

The overall picture of electricity's efficiency and applications-diffusion development is that once the uncertainty surrounding electricity's viability was overcome, it was obvious to FPS agents that it had many profitable and fairly immediate applications. Originally, these were mostly in places where electricity was a close substitute for a power technology already in existence (e.g., steam power in manufacturing in urban centres). Yet even in exploiting these applications uncertainties remained for the FPS. The NPS actors who supported the development of rural electrification in the United States and elsewhere were motivated by a predicted social return that was substantially greater than the private return that was appropriable by the FPS. This social return included a belief that unexploited complementarities existed with electricity but these were not well understood or well formulated at the time rural electrification occurred. Electricity eventually came to have many profitable applications in technologies for which there was no close substitute and that remains the case today.

Lessons

1. The invention trajectory of electricity is a strong counterexample to the common view that the NPS had little influence on invention and early application trajectories of any technology before the late nineteenth century. Electricity had a centuries-long, mostly NPS-supported invention trajectory and not until the viability of the technology was proven did it gain significant FPS support.
2. The invention, efficiency, and applications-diffusion trajectories of the battery offer a similar refutation of the view that the NPS played little or no role in the development of technologies before the late nineteenth century. The invention of the battery also demonstrates the critical role the NPS played to help establish the viability of the technology and then an uptake by the FPS once the technology was proven.
3. The FPS and NPS sectors often work together, each contributing significantly to the final result.
4. The NPS can play a critical role in the early development of technologies where the exploitation of technological complementarities that relate to the technology cluster might seem unprofitable for agents in the FPS but are thought to have high potential social spillover. In these situations, FPS agents may never foresee sufficient profit to motivate investment even though there is significant socio-economic benefit to be derived in developing the technologies.
5. The NPS has an important part to play when a technology's profitable uses require a long period of changes in the capital goods that use it. Profitable opportunities typically only emerge after such changes have been made.

4.5.2 Computers and the Internet

Computers and the internet technologies stand in a hierarchy since computers were required for the invention of the Internet. Both depend on electricity. Important, both produce feedbacks for the other's applications as they coevolve. The NPS support for computers and the Internet has enabled massive opportunities in the applications trajectories of other technologies, including those that did not receive much direct NPS support themselves.

These two technologies are so intertwined that is it difficult to keep their stories separate. Nonetheless, we present our description of the invention, efficiency, and applications trajectories of the computer and the Internet separately and gather the lessons from both at the end of the section.

Computers

We use the term *computer* to refer to the generic technology cluster of electronic computing and regard the Internet, one of its major applications, as a separate technology although Carlaw, Lipsey, and Webb (2007) treat the two as a single technology cluster of networked, flexible programmable logic.[27] Computers are systems of flexible programmable logic that reside in combinations of hardware and software that have coevolved in complex ways in their efficiency and applications-diffusion trajectories. These systems are based on such technologies and principles as electricity, mathematics, mechanics, and logic. Their major functions are the generalised creation, communication, storage, and manipulation of information.

Invention Trajectory

Several FPS-funded mechanical computing devices were predecessors of the electronic computer, including the textile loom controlled by paper punch cards invented by Joseph Marie Jacquard, Herman Hollerith's data-recording device, and Charles Babbage's Analytical Engine, which has been described as Turing Complete (functional program-controlled) (Bromley, 1990). Babbage did not complete this and others of his calculating machines due to inadequate financing. The invention of the electronic computer and its technological complements were almost entirely financed by the NPS.

---

[27] Carlaw, Lipsey, and Webb (2007) treat the computer and the Internet as the same technology, which they refer to as Programmable Computing Networks (PCN). While at some level of abstraction this treatment makes sense, it is common practice to treat these technologies separately, and we do so here.

The 'Turing Machine'[28] was a device Alan Turing conceptualised in 1936 while he was studying at Princeton University. It outlined the central concept of the modern computer. Other early work was done by George R. Stibitz during the period 1937–42 when he made his major contributions while working at Bell Labs. Among other things, he was the first to use binary relays and Boolean logic.

There were several inventions shortly after Turing's initial conjectures. All of the work on these was largely NPS-funded, military investment forming a large part of the PPS/NEO component. These include the Atanasoff-Berry computer, created in 1937 by John Vincent Anastoff and his graduate student Clifford Berry at Iowa State College. It was funded by NGO support in the form of a grant from the agronomy department at Iowa State University (Petersen, 2002: 74). Anastoff worked with the US Army during World War II (Campbell-Kelly & Aspray, 1996: 84). In Germany, Konrad Zuse invented the first Turing complete computer in 1941, called the Z3. His research was mostly financed by his family but did eventually garner some PPS support from the Nazi government (O'Regan, 2008: 69–70; Weiss, 1996: 3). Prior to World War II, Turing was employed by the British Government Code and Cypher School, which was located at Bletchley Park from 1939 throughout World War II.[29] It was here that Turing, with British government finance, created first a mechanical computer in 1940, then the electronic Colossus computer in 1943. Both of these secret British government computers were used in breaking the German Enigma wartime code (Campbell-Kelly & Aspray, 1996). The Harvard Mark I was conceived of by Howard Aiken, funded and built by IBM in 1944, then sent to Harvard University in 1944 (Campbell-Kelly & Aspray, 1996: 69). The ENIAC, built by the US Army's Ballistic Research Laboratory in 1946, is considered by many to be the first electronic computer, although both Turing's and Zuse's predated it. The probable reason is that the existence of Turing's Colossus was unknown for a long time after the war due to the British government's secrecy regarding all of its code-breaking successes while knowledge of Zuse's computer was obscured by the defeat of Germany.

These early computers all had inflexible architectures limiting them to dealing only with the problem for which they were wired. A fundamental breakthrough came with a new design known as stored program architecture that was first described formally by John von Neumann. While the computation

---

[28] The 'Turing Machine' was not an actual computer but a conceptual device (Hopcroft, 1984) described in a paper Turing published in 1936.

[29] The Government Code and Cypher School was created at the end of World War I and originally housed at University of Cambridge and the National Physical Laboratory, University of Manchester.

methods were hardwired, the data and instructions for each specific job were inputted separately, giving the machine the flexibility needed to tackle a vast number of different jobs. Several versions of the stored-program-architecture computer were built virtually simultaneously and all were almost completely financed by the NPS.[30] The first fully operational stored-program computer in the United States was the SEAC built by the National Bureau of Standards in 1950 (Langlois & Mowery, 1996: 11). The IAS computer built in 1951 by von Neumann at the Institute for Advanced Study was funded by various PPS and FPS sources, including the US Army, the US Navy, and the Radio Corporation of America (RCA) (Langlois & Mowery, 1996: 11).

Efficiency Trajectory

Hardware The early efficiency gains for the electronic computer were in some instances financed mainly by the NPS and in others by a mixture of the NPS and the FPS, such as in the case of Bell Labs.

> During World War II, Bell Laboratories undertook more than 2000 research projects for the Army, Navy, and the National Defense Research Council. Between 1949–1959, the U.S. Government funded more than $600 million of research at Western Electric and Bell Laboratories (approximately 50% of [the] total Research Budget of Bell Laboratories.) During this period the Department of Defense allocated between $1 million and $2 million annually to over one hundred doctoral candidates working on basic research of solid-state physics. (Lojek, 2007: 11)

Bell Labs is an entity that is difficult to classify in our categories. It enjoyed a mix of FPS and PPS financial support and was driven sometimes by scientific curiosity, sometimes by profit motive, and sometimes by military engineering requirements. It is difficult to identify in this history what portions of the research were NPS and FPS financed because of the nature and sources of financing in Bell Labs. It is clear that by the time many of its patents were issued, the commercial value of the innovations had become obvious to and in most cases claimed by FPS interests. What is also clear is that there was a cooperative NPS and FPS effort. Bell Labs during this period represents the

---

[30] These include the Manchester Mark I built by the Victoria University of Manchester, the Electronic Delay Storage Automatic Calculator built at Cambridge University, and the Electronic Discrete Variable Automatic Computer (EDVAC), which used binary rather than decimal machine language and was built for the US Army's Ballistic Research Laboratory by the University of Pennsylvania's Moore School of Electrical Engineering (Campbell-Kelly & Aspray, 1996: chapter 4).

epitome of this cooperation in technology development. (See the Appendix for more detail on this important facility.)

One of the most important early efficiency gains came with the invention of the transistor in 1947–8 by several engineers and physicists in Europe and at Bell Labs. The European developments appear to have been largely FPS financed. Prominent among the Europeans we identify in the FPS was Julius Lilienfeld, who invented something close to a field-effect transistor (FET) and took out several patents, one of which was in Canada in 1925 (Kleint, 1998: 256, 314). Oskar Heil was also an early European FPS pioneer in transistor research. He took out a patent on 'Improvements in, or relating to, electrical amplifiers and other control arrangements and devices' which was regarded as a breakthrough in FETs (Sarkar, Khan & Basumallick, 2007: 340–1). Herbert Franz Mataré was in the NPS at the Technical University of Aachen and University of Geneva when he developed a functional 'European' transistor in 1948 independently of the Bell Labs engineers (van Dormael, 2009: 68).

In the United States, John Bardeen won two Nobel Laureates, one for the transistor and one for theories concerning superconductivity, which he developed while working at Bell Labs (Hoddeson & Dautch, 2002). Walter Brattain and William Shockley both won Nobel Prizes for their separate work on the transistor (Lojek, 2007: 12). Bardeen, Brattain, and Shockley appear to have been motivated (at least in part) by considerations other than profit, publishing their work in scientific journals, but Bell Labs was quick to take out patents on their work. Gordon Teal refined the silicon transistor. Teal and Morgan Sparks successfully fabricated the first working junction transistor from a germanium crystal in April 1950 (Riordan, 2004: 46). Later, Teal, with the help of technician Ernie Buehler, grew single crystals of silicon and used them to make solid-state diodes (Riordan, 2004: 46). M. M. (John) Atalla joined the considerable Bell Labs transistor effort in 1956 as a supervisor. His work there on electromagnetic relays led to an early version of a metal-oxide-semiconductor (MOS) transistor (Bassett, 2002: 22). It seems that the original concepts for MOS and integrated circuits were co-developed by several researchers working at Bell Labs prior to the issue of several patents related to these innovations. In 1959, Atalla and Dawon Kahng began work on an MOS structure at Bell Labs (Bassett, 2002: 24). The MOS transistor was significantly different from the bipolar transistor originally developed by Shockley and his team at Bell Labs. However, the management at Bell Labs halted the work on the MOS transistor, 'dismissing it as unpromising' (Bassett, 2002: 13). Very soon, FPS firms such as RCA and Fairchild saw the promise of MOS and devoted significant R&D to its development (Bassett, 2002: 13).

Another important early efficiency development was the integrated circuit. This had many antecedents which included the idea to integrate several transistors onto one chip for which a patent application was made by Bernard M. Oliver in 1952 when he was working at Bell Labs. Then, in 1953, Harwick Johnson, who worked for the FPS institution RCA, described a 'Semiconductor Phase Shift Oscillator and Device' that later obtained a patent which was basically an integrated circuit (Lojek, 2007: 2).

The early development of the integrated circuit is usually attributed to Robert Noyce, Jean Hoerni, Kurt Lehovee, and Jack Kilby. The Nobel Prize was later awarded to Kilby for his part in the invention of the circuit. Although they all worked at Bell Labs at the time their ideas were being developed and published in NPS scientific journals, the patent was subsequently granted to a private firm, Fairchild, at the time Kilby was working for Texas Instruments (Lojek, 2007: 176). Texas Instrument's president, Patrick E. Haggerty, aggressively pursued sales of 'Solid Circuits' to the US Air Force and ended up beating out Fairchild by obtaining a major military contract to build integrated circuits in 1961 (Lojek, 2007: 192).

Software Software, a program stored in the memory of a digital computer, came into existence in its modern form when computers ceased to be hardwired to solve specific problems and, following von Neumann's insights, became general-purpose programmable computers. Before that, the first theory concerning software was developed in the NPS by Alan Turing in his 1936 essay 'Computable Numbers'. Like hardware, the initial development of software was financed with a mixture of NPS and FPS support.

Post–World War II efforts to develop software relied to a great extent on university researchers (Langlois & Mowery, 1996: 5). The NPS support remained important in many software advances from the mid 1950s onwards. For example, John W. Tukey, who enjoyed NGO support and was credited with coining the term 'software' was a professor of mathematics at Princeton for his entire career. He also held a senior position in the Department of Statistics and Data Analysis at Bell Labs. He made several mathematical contributions to software development such as the fast Fourier transform and the box plot. The contributions of US universities to the developments of this period and later relied on the extremely important growth of the new academic discipline of computer science. The creation of this academic field was aided by PPS support during the 1950s and 1960s for the purchase of mainframe computers that were essential to its creation and development (Langlois & Mowery, 1996: 5).

Numerous military procurement contracts greatly contributed to software standardisation. For example, in 1960, the US DoD financed the creation of the programming language COBOL, which facilitated the replacement of magnetic tape drives and enabled one form of standardisation for programing languages (Robinson & Cargill, 1996: 82). Using this PPS/NEO-funded project, an FPS project at General Electric headed by Charles Bachman created the integrated data store (IDS) system (NRSC, 1999: 161). From this followed the development of standardisation for the navigation of databases that became known as Codasyl. By 1996, COBOL had become a popular program for business applications with 17 billion lines in use (Robinson & Cargill, 1996: 82–3).

In 1974, the DoD appointed a committee to determine the requirements for a unified programming language and to evaluate the suitability of existing languages. Mistakenly believing that no suitable language existed, the DoD contracted Honeywell Bull to create the ADA programming language (Langlois & Mowery, 1996: 52–3). ADA was announced in 1981 and became required in all major DoD procurements. A drawback of this was that ADA had few civilian applications and therefore did not facilitate commercial spin-offs (Langlois & Mowery, 1996: 52–3). In the years following the implementation of ADA, the Joint Services Task Force published a report advising the DoD to bridge the gap between civilian and military applications (Langlois & Mowery, 1996: 54–5). However, this gap was never successfully bridged. ADA was never the commercially successful standardisation COBOL was.

A key difference between the history of COBOL and ADA was that COBOL was developed by a joint collaboration between the DoD and commercial interests at a pre-commercial stage, while ADA was developed after the DoD had already created a software standard success with COBOL. The top-down decision process concerning ADA occurred at the stage when the commercial viability of COBOL and FORTRAN were being proved.[31] Thus there was no need for the DoD to pursue ADA. It was not commercially successful partly because COBOL was already commercially viable and available, and partly because it was designed specifically for the military, not for commercial spin-off (Langlois & Mowery, 1996: 54–5).

Another example of PPS-supported software development is found in the various protocols developed for the DoD by interconnected academic institutions under the umbrella of ARPANET for what would become the Internet. We say more about this in our discussion of the Internet.

---

[31] The development of FORTRAN was FPS funded, intended by IBM as a replacement for assembly language (Mindell, 2008).

One key point from the preceding discussion is that significant amounts of PPS funding were put into various software developments which produced two major trajectories of exploitable complementarities. One trajectory was an infrastructure of academic experts, built largely with government funding; the other was the establishment of high and uniform industry standards such as COBOL. These PPS/NEO-funded standards influenced and aided the development of FPS-funded software production.

Applications-Diffusion Trajectory

Many applications of the computer were supported by the PPS via NEO, military procurement or EO, or direct government programmes during the early stages of the development of its hardware and software efficiency. There are of course many other applications of the computer that have in the past and continue to enjoy varying degrees of NPS support. Many of these applications, such as biotechnology and nanotechnology, are themselves major technologies into which the technologies of electricity, computers, and the Internet have become background components. This Element touches only tangentially on these other important applications of the computer. However, by far one of the most important of these applications was the Internet. Although this technology is one of the computer's myriad applications, we treat the Internet as a stand-alone technology. We then gather together the lessons learned from the computer and the Internet at the end of this section.

Internet

The Internet is an electronic network that interconnects and includes at its core the computer plus all electronic information networks that use flexible machine logic such as local area networks (LANs), wide area networks (WANs), and wireless networks.

Invention Trajectory

In an early example of remote manipulation of flexible logic, George Stibitz (PhD mathematics, Cornell University) remotely operated the IBM Model 1 computer via telephone wire at Bell Laboratories in 1940 (Winston, 1998: 322). In an early example of PPS-supported activity, Vannevar Bush of the US Office of Scientific Research and Planning published an article in 1945 describing a machine that 'allows for the entire compendium of human knowledge to be accessed or searched in an associative manner' (Winston, 1998: 322).

In the United States, military sources were the largest historical funder of the Internet and of the post-war development of the computer more generally

(Flamm, 1988). Development efforts were also widely dispersed through academic/research institutions and industry partnerships, often with financial backing from the military.

In 1946, the US Air Force founded RAND, 'a nonprofit corporation dedicated to research on military strategy and technology' (Abbate, 2000: 10). In 1950, the US Congress established the National Science Foundation (NSF) to fund basic research, especially in universities (NRCS, 1999: 12). These two initiatives formed the foundation of support for what was to become the Internet.

A forerunner of the Internet in the United States was the PPS-funded SAGE 'computer', which began operating as a research programme in 1954 for the US Air Force. It comprised twenty-six interconnected computing modules that effectively represented the first LAN. It involved MIT, Bell Labs, AT&T, IBM, the Burroughs Corporation, and the RAND Corporation. By 1963, there were twenty-four SAGE Direction Centers and three SAGE Combat Centers, each connected by long-distance telephone wires to more than one hundred interoperating air defence elements (SAGE, 2005). This level of system communication and integration was so large that its development gave AT&T a significant lead in high-speed communication and modem technology, which AT&T had been instrumental in developing for the SAGE programme (Flamm, 1988).

One major funding source for the Internet (and many other technologies) was the Advanced Research Projects Agency (ARPA). It was established by the US DoD in 1958 under pressure by the Eisenhower administration to respond to the Russian launching of Sputnik II. The ARPA's mandate was to 'fund technological projects with military implications' (NRCS, 1999: 13).

> [Ninety per cent] of all good things that I can think of that have been done in computer science have been funded by [ARPA] ... The basic ARPA idea is that you find good people, give them a lot of money and step back. If they don't do good things in three years, they get dropped.[32]

The Internet's development was initiated by ARPA in 1966 under the programme name ARPANET to investigate interlinked packet networks. The project's goal was to create a network that could link autonomous computers together from a variety of terminal nodes. This ultimately resulted in the TCP/IP Protocol Suite. The project continued through 1986 with the US National Science Foundation's (NSF) initiation of the development of the NSFNET (currently providing the major communication architecture service for the Internet), and was supported by communication facilities contributed by NASA and the US Department of Energy (NRCS, 1999: 78).

---

[32] Alan Kay, on the US Department of Defense's Advanced Projects Research Agency (ARPA) (Rao & Scaruffi, 2013).

Networks that predate or co-date with ARPANET which were formative for the Internet and which were NPS supported include Merit Network, CSNET, NSFNET, CYCLADES, SERCnet (later JANET), and International Packet Switched Service (IPSS). Merit Network, which was NGO funded, was established in 1966 as a consortium of public universities (Michigan State, University of Michigan, and Wayne State University) and successfully completed its first network in 1972 (Aupperle, 1998). It played a major early role in the development of critical network technologies in the United States that would culminate in the modern Internet, including CSNET and NSFNET.

CSNET was funded by the NSF for three years from 1981 to 1984. Its purpose was to extend network computing benefits to emerging computer science departments at academic and research institutions that could not get access to ARPANET (Comer 1983). This network was linked into the Merit network. It was the forerunner to the National Science Foundation Network (NSFNET), which is widely considered the precursor of the modern Internet. NSFNET was funded by the NSF and began in 1985. It was a coordinated collection of programmes to support advanced research and education networking which coevolved to eventually become the backbone of the Internet (Schuster, 2016).

CYCLADES, which was PPS funded by the French government and housed at Institut de Recherche en Informatique et en Automatique (IRIA), completed a packet-switched network in 1973 (Kim, 2005). SERCnet was based on a packet-switching software, X.25, developed by the NGO International Telecommunications Union (a United Nations special agency for information and communications technologies). X.25 itself was based on ARPANET's packet-switching standards. SERCnet linked British universities and research centres. International Packet Switched Service (IPSS) was a collaboration between the PPS and FPS entities of the British Postal Service, Western Union International, and Tymnet.

This list is merely representative of a large number of early networks that evolved out of NPS-supported activities. Universities and research laboratories were eager to link their communications together in the early development stages of the Internet. The large list of interrelated networks and the nature of the Internet also make it difficult to identify where the invention trajectory of the Internet ends and the efficiency and applications-diffusion trajectories begin. And as Carlaw, Lipsey, and Webb (2007) note, the Internet is in some sense just a scaled-up version of the information-processing and transmission activities of computers with the addition of packet-switching protocols to handle the disintegration and reintegration of information. Noting the lack of an obvious and agreed date, we place the end of the Internet's invention trajectory in the period between the late 1970s and early 1980s. At this point, there were many emerging autonomous networks that were coevolving and converging with the development of standardised formal and widely adopted TCP and then TCP/IP. (Some observers place the invention date in 1983, when ARPANET formally adopted TCP/IP.)

Efficiency and Applications-Diffusion Trajectories

The efficiency and applications-diffusion trajectories of the Internet reveal a complementary coevolution of the trajectories of several technologies, most notably the computer, telecommunications and satellite technology, computer software specific to the Internet (e.g., TCP/IP and ethernet IP), and applications software (e.g., STMP for email and web browsers). Although we do not go into great detail on some of these linkages here (e.g., PPS support for specific telecommunications technologies), we do link some of the developments of the Internet to the development of some of these separately identifiable technologies as we proceed through the discussion of the Internet.

Several researchers funded by NPS at RAND developed various aspects of the theory of packet switching which led the ARPA to fund the construction of a prototype network (Fabrizio & Mowery, 2007: 305).[33] Around the same time, Donald Davies of the PPS-funded National Physics Laboratory in the UK produced his own version of packet switching. The results of this work and the work at RAND were subsequently provided to Lawrence Roberts, who was in charge of creating ARPANET during 1967–9 (Abbate, 2000: 8; NRCS, 1999: 172). This was the US Military's original version of the Internet and the origin of TCP/IP protocols.

From the outset, virtually all the developments of the Internet were supported by NPS and often occurred in joint research-procurement projects among government research agencies often housed in universities or industrial laboratories, military departments, and private companies. In 1991, the World Wide Web was established with the creation of HTML and HTTP by Tim Berners-Lee and Robert Cailliau, two physicists of a PPS-funded NGO, the Conseil européen pour la recherche nucléaire (CERN) laboratory, in Switzerland (Fabrizio & Mowery, 2007: 308).[34] At the same time, the US government introduced the PPS-funded High Performance Computing Act and the beginnings of Java created by SUN Microsystems. These developments stimulated the worldwide explosive growth of the Internet (Kleinrock, Khan & Clark, 1988).

With the existence of the World Wide Web, 1992 saw the beginnings of the explosive commercialisation of the Internet. Congressman Rich Boucher

---

[33] In the early 1970s, the ARPA was renamed the Defense Advanced Research Projects Agency (DARPA).

[34] The acronyms represent Hypertext Transfer Protocol (HTTP) and Hypertext Markup Language (HTML).

introduced an amendment to legislation authorising the NSF to support the development of computer systems for uses other than research and education (Ceruzzi, 2003: 322). In 1993, a group of graduate students at the NGO-funded University of Illinois National Center for Supercomputing Applications developed a free Internet browser called Mosaic (NRSC, 1999: 180). From this point on, web browser development expanded rapidly, largely supported by FPS financing.[35] The transformation of the Internet into commercially viable applications has been exploding since that time. Although NPS support has continued to develop infrastructure and bandwidth to encourage access, FPS-supported innovation has largely been driving applications development.

Lessons

1. The experiences of the computer and the Internet illustrate the enormous power of a workable cooperation between the NPS and the FPS in the development of new science-based technologies. Bell Labs provides an example of a particular form of this cooperation.
2. Top-down PPS directives that seek to manage and control the detailed development of a research programme do not typically generate either commercial successes or positive social spillovers, as illustrated by comparing the histories of COBOL and ADA.
3. NPS support for specific technologies often opens up massive spillovers that create opportunities in the applications trajectories of other technologies, including those that did not receive much direct NPS support themselves. In such cases, the social returns to the NPS support of the original technologies must be calculated as more than just marginal rates of return to the specific investments targeted, or even positive externalities conferred on third parties. Instead, the social value of these NPS actions must be understood in terms of broad spillovers which may include developments based on myriad technological complementarities created by the original development and extending over years or even decades.

4.5.3 Lasers

The precursor of the laser was the maser. A maser is a device that produces coherent electromagnetic waves through amplification by stimulated emission. The word 'maser' is derived from the acronym MASER: 'Microwave

---

[35] The large list of early commercial web browsers includes Mosaic, Netscape, Netscape Navigator, Microsoft Windows Internet Explorer, America On Line's (AOL) internal browser, and so forth (Berners-Lee, 2010).

Amplification by Stimulated Emission of Radiation'. A laser is a device that emits light through a process of optical amplification based on the stimulated emission of electromagnetic radiation. The term 'laser' originated as an acronym for 'Light Amplification by Stimulated Emission of Radiation'. Lasers differ from other sources of light because they emit light coherently. Spatial coherence allows a laser to be focussed to a tight spot, enabling applications like laser cutting and lithography. Spatial coherence also allows a laser beam to stay narrow over long distances, enabling applications such as laser pointers. The main difference between lasers and masers is that lasers use light and masers use microwaves.

The Invention Trajectory

The initial motivation for the invention of both the maser and the laser was a combination of scientific curiosity and hope that the technologies might have application as military weapons of a type called direct energy weapons.[36] Although scholars disagree about who ought to receive credit for the invention of the maser and the laser, they do agree about who funded it. Almost all of the funding for the R&D on both the maser and the laser came from the PPS, largely from US military defense contracts and from the Soviet and British governments. This research began near the end of World War II and continued through the Cold War period (Bromberg, 1986). During that time, militaries in these countries were interested in finding new technologies related to weapons and communications and masers and lasers were seen as possibilities. Scientists in the laboratories of private companies and universities were funded in hopes of developing the best new technologies.

The 1950s was an era of continued significant PPS funding from predominantly military sources that helped to create a significant R&D infrastructure in the United States (Bromberg 1986: 2).[37] Much of this was devoted to the invention and development of the maser and the laser. In 1954, at the Columbia Radiation Laboratory of Columbia University, Charles Townes and Arthur Schawlow, supported by $500,000 in PPS funding from the Joint Services Electronics Project (JSEP), developed the ammonia maser. Soviet scientists Nikolay Basov and Aleksandr Prokhorov also performed PPS-funded research that contributed to the invention of the maser and laser,

---

[36] Direct energy weapons as a concept goes back at least to Nikola Tesla (Seifer, 1988). This type of weapon includes lasers, sonic weapons, electromagnetic weapons, and heat weapons. For the most part, this line of military research appears to have been unfruitful, although it did generate several unforeseen applications such as laser-guided missiles and drones.

[37] The DoD spending on R&D rose from $590 million in 1948 to $2.6 billion in 1956 (Bromberg, 1986: 2).

independently of Townes. They shared the 1964 Nobel Prize in Physics with Townes (Shampo, Kyle & Steensma, 2012: 3). The JESP also supported maser and laser programmes at other universities and industrial research laboratories throughout the 1950s (Bromberg, 1986: 2). The availability of military research funding spawned the birth of several industrial laboratories which were often supported by mixes of NPS and FPS financing (Bromberg, 1986: 2).[38] In this way, PPS funding supported not only the direct innovations of the maser and laser, it also supported innovations in organisational technologies. These created collaborations among private firms, universities, the military, and other researchers which resulted in the research hybrid of the industrial research laboratory. This cooperative mixture is a story we have seen repeatedly in the development of the Internet and other computer software, aircraft, steamships, and so forth.

Hughes Research and Development Laboratories (HRDL), an important and already established defense contractor, also wanted to pursue maser development because of the maser's possible ability to guide missiles (Bromberg, 1986: 26). Scientists originally at Harvard Radio Research Laboratory and Columbia University formed a commercial firm and in 1955 obtained a contract from the US Air Force to build an ammonia beam maser. Bell Telephone and RCA Laboratories also began maser research. RCA was backed by the Army Signal Corps due especially to the presence of its most important scientist, Robert H. Dicke, who had previously been funded by the Corps outside of RCA. As a leader in American communications, Bell was also interested in the maser due to its possible communications applications (Bromberg, 1986: 27, 29).

Military contracts were awarded to universities and private companies alike and, though the physicists involved may have been motivated by pure scientific curiosity, almost all of their key breakthroughs were supported by PPS funds. The military provided the equipment to test and build new technologies and incentives through its suggestions for maser applications and its granting of prestige to those in the field (Hecht, 2005: 73–4). Most important, by awarding financing to talented individuals, the military enabled future developments, including the laser (Hecht, 2005: 73–4).

By the mid to late 1950s, Schawlow and Townes were developing their paper on optical masers and Gordon Gould was moving forward with his own ideas on the subject. In 1958, Gould was hired by the PPS-funded Technical Research Group (TRG), a company whose early contracts were with DoD agencies such

---

[38] The number of industrial laboratories grew from approximately three thousand to fifty-four hundred between 1950 and 1960 (Bromberg, 1986: 2).

as the Office of Naval Research, the Air Force Cambridge Research Center, and the John Hopkins Applied Physics Laboratory (Bromberg, 1986: 74). A former president and one of the founders of TRG, Lawrence Goldmuntz, stated during an interview that if you approached the government with a good proposal they would generally support it (Bromberg, 1986: 74). The labs previously mentioned in the undertaking of maser research also engaged in laser research. The main researchers included staff at Columbia and Harvard Universities, Bell, IBM, Hughes, Westinghouse Labs, and the American Optical Company, all supported by NGO funding.

Townes (working at Columbia) applied for and received PPS funding in 1958 from the Air Force Office of Scientific Research to allow him to attempt to build a potassium laser (Bromberg, 1986: 78). In a separate line of enquiry, TRG supported Gould's ideas and approached ARPA for $300,000 in NEO funding to pursue laser research. ARPA actually provided almost $1 million (Hecht, 2005: 83). However, there was a catch to these funds. The problem with some government military contracts is that they are often declared secret. This was the case with TRG's contract. The whole project was declared classified and could not be discussed outside TRG. This in itself was not a significant barrier. The biggest hurdle came when Gould, the key idea man charged with supervising and overseeing laser research, was not granted security clearance. He could not effectively participate in his own research. Federal agents actually confiscated Gould's own notebooks, classified them, and forbade him to see them due to his lack of security clearance. This secrecy became a huge hindrance to Gould and TRG.

Irwin Wieder at Westinghouse was also backed by NEO funding in the form of air force contracts during the development of the maser and these funds continued to help in the race to develop a working laser. Wieder helped others in the race by sharing his findings with them (Hecht, 2005: 90–2).

The real breakthrough occurred at Hughes, where Teddy Maiman created the first working laser in 1960. This research was made possible by NEO funding. Maiman had already built a ruby maser at Hughes aided by Army Signal Corps funding (Hecht, 2005: 107).

Efficiency

From its initial development, laser R&D increased rapidly in the United States, Europe, and the Soviet Union, and the military's interest continued to increase. Swift advancements in the laser field ensued, including the creation of a glass laser (Bromberg, 1991: 97). All these innovations continued to be PPS funded. Joan Bromberg estimates that the DoD spent approximately $1.5 million in 1960, $4 million in 1961, $12 million in 1962, and between $19 and $24 million by 1963 on laser R&D (Bromberg, 1991: 102). Universities and industry were also heavily supported by NEO funding. From 1961 to 1963, 80 per cent of papers related to lasers that were listed in *Physics Abstracts* and that originated from a university stated that they were supported by the DoD. It is also estimated that in 1962, more than seventy-five laser projects in the industrial sector obtained funds from the US military. By 1963, 130 contracts from the military were supporting the laser industry (Bromberg, 1991: 102). For example, once Maiman had created a working ruby laser, the Air Force awarded Hughes and Maiman more funds so they were free to develop bigger and better lasers (Bromberg, 1991: 194).

Most of the ongoing research on the laser performed in the Soviet Union was housed in the P. N. Lebedev Physical Institute operated by the Russian Academy of Sciences (RAS). The funding for the RAS came from the federal budget of the Soviet Union and then the Russian Federation (Pokrovsky, 2013).

Scotland's laser industry began in the 1960s with two optical engineering companies, Barr & Stroud and Ferranti, whose research was largely NGO funded (Scottish Optoelectronics Association, 2010).[39] Universities funded by NGOs also entered the laser industry early; the laser physics group at St Andrews University was started in 1963 (Scottish Optoelectronics Association, 2010). In the 1970s, Heriot-Watt University of Edinburgh built the UK's first research park on an academic campus. Over the ensuing twenty-plus years, there was a focus on collaboration between public and private interests (NGOs), with both St Andrews University and Strathclyde University establishing research institutes that include academics and private researchers, all of which was mostly NGO funded (Scottish Optoelectronics Association, 2010).

As in Scotland, laser research in England started just a few years after the invention of the laser and was heavily NGO funded. Oxford Lasers was spun out of Oxford University in 1977. Alan F. Gibson started his research at the University of Essex in 1963, where he discovered the photon-drag effect (Loundon & Paige, 1991: 233).[40] Bradley and Key built a working neodymium glass laser and conducted theoretical research into the x-ray laser supported by NGO funding at London University and Queen's University at Belfast. The Central Laser Facility (CLF) built at the Rutherford Laboratory in 1975 was fully PPS funded by the Science Research Council. It served as a laboratory

---

[39] Notably, Barr & Stroud produced the first military laser rangefinder, just seven years after the invention of the laser. Its modern version is now fitted to every battle tank in Britain.

[40] The photon drag effect is a manifestation of radiation pressure. The main effect is the generation of currents or electric fields in semiconductors by the transfer of momentum from an incident light beam to the charge carriers (Gibson, Kimmitt & Walker, 1970).

space for university researchers such as Gibson, who left the University of Essex to head up the CLF (Key, 2006).

Applications-Diffusion

The laser was ultimately used in a wide variety of applications that were initially unforeseen. Although applications were developed almost immediately after Maiman's successful construction of a ruby laser in 1961, it took almost the entire decade of the 1970s before lasers 'moved in any great numbers out of the laboratory and into the market place' (Bromberg, 1986: 163). Many applications have emerged since.

From the outset, lasers fitted well into the existing facilitating structures of most developed economies, which had already been heavily altered in response to the introduction of the computer. In many cases, lasers became complements to the computer and the Internet. Many of the laser's initial applications required public support because they did not have obvious commercial applications. But many of the laser's later developments simply made existing comerical applications more efficient and were developed by the FPS.

Communications Early interest was shown in the use of lasers for targeted optical communications, but the discovery that atmospheric interference significantly degrades beam coherence dampened hopes for terrestrial applications (Bertolotti, 2004). Although military (NEO) funding for space-based, beam applications of optical communications continued for some time (Hecht, 2005), FPS funding focussed on fibre-optics applications of the laser for communications. Aside from the challenges of manufacturing glass fibers of sufficient clarity, fibre optics also require a low-power, continuous light source (Hecht, 2005). For a variety of reasons, including compactness and solid-state materials, semiconductor/ diode lasers (SCL) proved ideal (Hecht, 2005: 147). After the initial principles were worked out by an NPS-funded team at MIT, two FPS-funded teams, from General Electric and IBM, worked to build prototypes (Hecht, 2005: 150). The technical challenges that emerged after the construction of early models, including beam coherence, temperature control, and lifespan, were largely resolved in the FPS by companies such as AT&T (Bell Labs) and General Electric (Hecht, 2005: 147). However, the Russians were the first to construct an NPS-funded room-temperature semiconductor laser, which was unknown in the West for some time due to publication restrictions behind the Iron Curtain. In the United States, the creation of fibre optic networks was funded largely by the aforementioned

FPS firms, although numerous other small firms in the FPS created small, local networks (Hecht, 2005: 274). In other countries, NPS organisations played a larger role – for example, the UK Post Office, the Nippon Telephone and Telegraph Company in Japan, and France Telecom (Hecht, 2005: 274). Thus, while the vast majority of funding for the application of laser technologies via fibre-optics communication networks in the United States originated in the FPS, there was great NPS support in other countries.

Medical The surgical use of lasers is now standard in numerous subfields, including cardiology, dermatology, neurosurgery, ophthalmology, and urology. The first applications of lasers in a medical context were mainly NPS supported but once the laser was proven as a commercially viable technology for medical applications, these were mostly FPS funded.

The application of lasers in ophthalmology originated in photocoagulation experiments on rabbits by Charles J. Campbell of the Columbia-Presbyterian Medical Center funded by the American Optical Company in 1961. The first human trials were performed by Milton Flocks and Christian Zweng of Stanford University in association with Narinder Kapany who founded Optics Technology Inc. The first commercially available photocoagulators were released in 1963 by Optics Technology and the American Optical Company in collaboration with academic researchers and with funding from the NIH. Between 1965 and 1969, Francis L'Esperance of the Columbia-Presbyterian Medical Center worked with Bell Labs to utilise the newly developed argon laser for photocoagulation. He received $287,000 in funding from an NGO, the John A. Hartford Foundation, to start the work. Coherent Incorporated brought the subsequent designs to market in 1969, which became the standard in the field (Gelijns & Rosenberg, 1995: 52–3).

Outside of ophthalmology, the pioneering of medicinal laser applications was done by Leon Goldman of the University of Cincinnati (Geiges, 2011). His research began in 1962 and was funded by the US Public Health Service, the National Institutes of Health (NIH), and the Hartford Foundation NGO (Spetz, 1995: 54). Goldman's labs at the university introduced dermatological procedures for tattoo removal, vascular lesions, and skin cancers, which work led to treatments for a wide variety of cutaneous lesions (Wheeland, 1995: 4). Starting in the 1970s, devices for these procedures began to be produced by companies such as Coherent Radiation, Optics Technology, Sharplan, and Cooper Labs. Endoscopic applications of lasers were developed and commercialised in the FPS sector in the late 1970s and 1980s by companies such as Coherent

Radiation, Trimedyne, and Laserscope. After the 1960s, 'Most of the research and development [for medical laser devices] received its funding from outside the public sector [i.e., were FPS funded] and entrepreneurial individuals sought venture capital for their ideas' (Spetz, 1995: 57).

Manufacturing From the mid 1960s through the 1970s and onward, there was an expansion out of scientific and industrial laboratories into manufacturing activities for applications of the laser. These were supported by both the FPS and the NPS. The Vietnam War accelerated applications for laser radars, target designators, and reconnaissance systems supported by NEO military procurement. Social concerns for the environment and the search for alternative energy sources through laser fusion led to more PPS support for research into applications. This time, other applications, such as systems for alignment and measurement as well as materials processing, were being developed by the FPS. The number of private firms manufacturing lasers rose from fewer than 20 in 1963 to about 115 in 1965. By 1964, it was clear laser technology had been sufficiently proven to warrant significant FPS investment into its applications. However, the major migration of lasers out of the publicly funded research laboratory and into the industrial marketplace took nearly two decades (Bromberg, 1986: 162–3).

Retail The first supermarket laser scanning system was developed by Spectra Physics in the FPS and implemented at a Marsh supermarket in Ohio. Such systems were developed independently by Phillips and Sony in 1969, with additional developments by MCA and RCA as well (Bertolotti, 2004; Hecht, 2010). By 1980, they had become commonplace (Gill, 2000; Hecht, 2010). However, an important feature of these early applications of lasers that allowed them to become commonplace was the development of the standardisation of barcodes, which required PPS support. These codes enable traceability on a global scale, which allows data to pass smoothly down the supply chain and enables consumers to access data about products (GS1, 2016: 6–19).

Major network externalities were associated with the needed standardisation of barcodes, and these were exploited with NGO support. GS1 is a largely PPS-funded international organisation in charge of the standardisation of barcode readings that arose when several organisations joined together, one of which was the Electronic Commerce Council of Canada (ECCC). The role GS1 played in standardising was critical in exploiting the massive network externalities that exist in product code marking and tracking. GS1's PPS support enabled it to overcome the fixed costs of standardisation that the member firms could not finance individually. By bringing these private interests together and using PPS support to cover the fixed costs, the public-good problem was overcome. Barcode standardisation then occurred to the benefit of everyone in the network.

Lessons

1. Because, as we have observed, technological innovation is an uncertain evolutionary process, PPS support often produces unforeseen and huge socio-economic benefits, both when the original project fails, as with the laser, and when it succeeds, as with many other projects.
2. The value of FPS and NPS cooperation is well illustrated by the laser, which was created and developed during the Cold War. Diverse scientific expertise was mobilised and focussed on several different projects, such as lasers, telecommunications, computers, and the Internet, that were related through their technological complementarities. These projects were PPS funded (often for military purposes) under broad research umbrellas that brought together university, military, other government and commercial research expertise. The combining of these diverse resources served to enable the development of the laser and its many complementary, commercially valuable applications.
3. Major new technologies are often opposed by some agents in the economy because they appear to be (and often are) disruptive or even destructive. When these technologies emerge, many destroy much of the value of existing parts of the facilitating structure and cut off the development of new parts associated with the old technologies that the new displaces. The experience of the computer, which displaced old systems of information and communication management and organisation, illustrates that such opposition is not typically justified. The computer ultimately brought massive new economic gains along with its significant displacements and disruptions. It is also worth noting that such displacements and disruptions do not necessarily occur with the emergence of all radical new technologies. The laser is an example of such a non-disruptive, radical, new technology that fitted well into the existing facilitating structure.

5 General Lessons

In the previous section, we offered specific lessons related to the individual technologies we have considered. Here, we offer general lessons that apply to many, sometimes all, of the technologies considered in this Element.

1. **The actions of agents in both the FPS and NPS influence the evolutionary trajectories of technologies. In some cases, the NPS agents need to provide a demonstration of a technology's viability ('proof of concept') before FPS agents are willing to finance further developments towards commercialisation. In other cases, the relationship operates in reverse, with the FPS agents demonstrating technological viability before the NPS is willing to finance a significant amount of the technology's further evolution.**

A contrast between two subsets of the cases in Groups 2, 3, and 4 in Table 1 illustrates this point. In the case of refrigeration (Group 2) and the jet engine (Group 3), the technology needed minimal NPS support to be proven viable in its invention trajectory before FPS agents were prepared to finance its widespread uptake and exploitation. In contrast, railways, automobiles, aircraft (in Group 3), and the iron steamship (Group 4) required that the FPS provide the initial demonstration of viability before NPS agents (often in the NEO sector) were willing to provide finance for many of the developments in the efficiency and applications-diffusion trajectories. An important question is, what are the conditions that favour each of the two causal sequences? Although we do not yet have a full answer, our research suggests some tentative ones.

Conditions favouring FPS first: there are established close substitutes to the emerging technology to which the NPS, often in the form of the military contracts, is heavily committed; the invention seems probable once sufficient R&D is directed to it; the applications are fairly obvious and offer profits over not-too-long time horizons; a well-developed facilitating structure exists that can easily be adapted to serve the new technology.

Conditions favouring NPS first: the invention phase is long drawn out and full of uncertainty, with the main research incentives being curiosity and fame rather than profit; once an initial breakthrough has been achieved, it is clear in a general way that there will be a massive number of direct applications and spillovers, but these are distant and uncertain in time and technological detail (as, e.g., when Crick and Watson made their original discovery of the nature of the hereditary mechanism); the motives for financing the R&D for the discovery phase come from non-economic objectives in the PPS sector, often the NEO; the major pay-offs, at least in the early stages of development, are in terms of externalities and social gains rather than appropriable profits (as with rural electrification); the early development of the technology requires major changes in the facilitating structure that are in the nature of non-appropriable public goods.

2. The more a technology depends on science, the larger the place for NPS support for the relevant trajectories.

The First Industrial Revolution was based mainly on Newtonian mechanics, while the second depended much more on modern science. From then on, science has played an increasingly important part in the various trajectories of new technologies. This has created a place for publicly financed research where the agents in the FPS were unwilling to finance it because of such impediments as: (i) a lack of foresight, (ii) inadequate financial incentives, (iii) an anticipated overly long invention trajectory, and (iv) a heavy concentration of the social pay-offs on externalities and broader spillovers, rather than profits for those directly involved in financing the various trajectories. The part played by the public sector has for these reasons grown steadily as new technologies have become increasingly complex and science based. Of the technologies considered in this Element, science played an important part in the efficiency and application-diffusion stages of the aircraft industry, particularly by the NACA in the United States; the Green Revolution in agriculture; the entire invention trajectory of electricity and somewhat in its later stages; and in all the trajectories of the computer, the Internet, and the laser. Some of those technologies not covered here in which NPS-financed science has played a major part, particularly in the early stages, are space travel, satellite communication, atomic power, biotechnology, and nanotechnology.

3. NPS support for emerging technologies can often remove some of the uncertainties that discourage FPS support.

This general lesson is closely related to Lesson 2. Much of the scientific understanding related to the pre-commercial development of a technology is generated in an environment of vast uncertainty. As noted in the introduction, because NPS financing has a different motivation and tolerance for uncertainty, it can provide a source of complementary financing to FPS investments at this early stage. Big technological leaps such as the development of the laser, computer, Internet, or the scientific understanding at the core of the Green Revolution require the sustained combination and coordination of large-scale financial and intellectual resources from many diverse sources, including universities, public and private research laboratories, private companies, and military engineers. The mechanisms that did this in the Cold War period of the 1950s and 1960s were mainly military procurement which combined public, private, and university (NGO) expertise in jointly FPS- and NPS-funded institutions such as Bell Labs. These provided a significant boost to the early development of technologies that were very large leaps into the unknown, starting from where scientific understanding was at the beginning of these endeavours.

4. **Being first mover in the development of some radical new technology that is replete with uncertainties can confer advantages but often provides the costly failures from which followers can learn.**

The de Havilland Comet and the Concord provide examples of the dangers of being first in such developments. For many of the technologies examined in this Element, this observation provides some of the rationale for cooperation between NPS and FPS agents. Often the process of development of major technological breakthroughs requires many 'failures' on the way to ultimate commercial success. The NPS-supported early developments of the computer, Internet, and lasers are cases in point. Many of the early stages of development of each of these technologies could not have been regarded as commercial successes by any FPS criteria, but they provided the necessary technological and scientific knowledge (both from failures and successes based on technological and scientific criteria) to develop the commercial successes built on the early endeavours. In contrast, many of the technologies that came to have NPS (particularly military procurement financing) support were first proven by FPS entrepreneurs. Our examples include iron steamships and early propeller aircraft and jets.

5. **Major technologies have significant coevolutionary complementarities among themselves. As a result, NPS support in the development trajectories of any one technology has significant positive and often difficult-sometimes-impossible-to-foresee, impacts, on the development trajectories of other technologies. These include some that were not directly supported by NPS themselves. NPS investments can also help to create positive feedbacks through these indirect impacts by creating further complementarities that subsequently affect the original technology. Thus, calculations of the 'return to NPS support' for a particular technology typically underestimate that return, unless they take account of the impact on the whole system of interconnected complementarities.**

Because Lesson 5 is important but complex, we illustrate it with several examples.

The internal combustion engine and transportation technologies: the internal combustion engine did not receive any significant, direct NPS support in its invention, efficiency, or applications-diffusion trajectories. It did, however, receive indirect support primarily in its applications-diffusion trajectory because the internal combustion engine became a central technology in the complex of

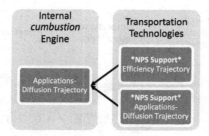

Figure 2 Simple indirect impact

interrelated transportation technologies of the automobile, railroads, ships, and aircraft. These transportation technologies all enjoyed significant NPS support in various forms and, in the case of aircraft, the transportation technology could not have existed without the internal combustion engine.[41] Furthermore, the internal combustion engine would have had significantly fewer and less pervasive applications had these technologies not been developed when and where they were. This was often with NPS support, sometimes directly, as with aircraft, and sometimes indirectly, as with the infrastructure that helped automobiles. Figure 2 illustrates the indirect impact of NPS support in transportation technologies on the applications of the internal combustion engine.

The internal combustion engine and refrigeration operating in conjunction with transportation technologies: NPS support for the invention trajectory of refrigeration had indirect impacts on the applications-diffusion trajectories of the internal combustion engine and transportation technologies for which it was critical in broadening their applications-diffusion trajectories. One example is found in vehicles with temperature control for passengers and cargo. In return, the applications-diffusion trajectory of refrigeration was broadened by the existence of the internal combustion engine and associated transportation technologies. Refrigeration on its own has many applications, but refrigeration combined with transportation technologies resulted in many more applications.

The lines in Figure 3 illustrate the complicated set of complementary relations among the technologies. The heavy solid lines represent complementarities operating in the direction of the arrow. The dashed lines represent two-way feedbacks. The light lines present complementarities running from an originating technology through and intermediate technology to an ultimate technology.

---

[41] Automobiles, railroads, and ships had versions of the technologies with alternative power technologies such as steam (and even electricity in the case of automobiles), but they all converged on the internal combustion engine as their power component in at least some versions, at some point in their development trajectories.

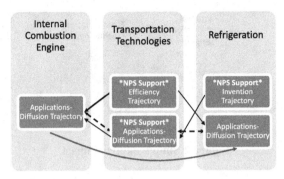

Figure 3 Complex indirect impact

Railroads: the NPS support enjoyed by railroads helped to expand the applications-diffusion trajectory of the steam engine and subsequently of the applications trajectories of the newer propulsion technologies of the diesel and electric motors.

As we have noted, NPS support for railroads also assisted the development of the applications and diffusion of such technologies as refrigeration and the telegraph.

The railroad also had far-reaching social and economic impacts. For example, by unifying the previously fractured US market, it allowed the exploitation of vast latent scale economies that led to the foundation of US dominance in manufacturing in the early twentieth century (Chandler, 1977: chapters 3 and 4; Rosenberg, 1982: chapter 3).

Automobiles: NPS support for automobiles along with NPS support for computers, lasers, and the Internet has enabled the co-development of, among other things, geographic information systems (GIS) for transportation and logistic control networks, and the emerging technologies of autonomous automobiles, transport trucks, and aircraft. This example illustrates how the original NPS support for the development of different technologies can have ongoing and unanticipated impacts on the exploitation of new technological opportunities that exist due to latent technological complementarities among the originally supported technologies.

In the cases of Japan and Korea, the complementary technologies of lean and 'just-in-time' production were developed and proven within the PPS-supported automobile manufacturing sector, but then this organisational technology spilled over to manufacturing activities in many other lines of production that benefitted from the original NPS investment in automobiles.

Aircraft: much of the economic impacts of NPS support for the various trajectories of aircraft technology has been manifested indirectly. This is true of the collection of identifiable technologies that assisted the efficiency trajectory of aircraft themselves, such as the NACA's wind tunnel. It is also true of the large collection of complementary technologies that worked with aircraft, such as airports, other transportation networks and infrastructure, and myriad other technologies that are linked to transportation systems including, for example, refrigeration for transportation of perishable goods.

Agriculture: the complementarity between agriculture and biotechnology is obvious, and the back-and-forth flow of ideas supported by NPS intervention is clear from the evolutionary history of both the development of such things as DNA sequencing and the Green Revolution.

The iron steamship: NPS support was important in developing and refining the cluster of steam power, screw propellers, and iron hulls. These were in turn linked to future technologies such as the internal combustion engine, which later substituted for steam but was itself complementary with screw propellers and iron and later steel hulls. Faster more reliable transoceanic transportation linked indirectly to almost everything else in terms of global transportation and trade networks. These later culminated in a linking to GIS and globalised container transportation which still uses steel hulls and screw propellers.

Electricity: electricity enables almost every technology currently in use. This can be seen either directly, as with every technology powered by it, or indirectly as with technologies that depend on it without being powered by it (e.g., manufactured goods made by electrically powered machine tools and chemical processes whose raw materials were created by electrically powered processes). In another area, NPS support for rural electrification enabled the development of a wide range of farming applications and opened up rural and agricultural demand for a range of existing and new technologies.

Computers and the Internet: these technologies stand in a hierarchy in that computers are required for the Internet while both require electricity. The NPS support for computers and the Internet has opened up massive opportunities in the applications trajectories of other technologies, including those that did not receive much direct NPS support themselves. Indeed, it is largely because of the computer and its derivatives that we live in an information and communications (ICT) age.

Lasers: NPS support existed for the development of the laser from the beginning of its invention trajectory right through its efficiency, development, and well into its applications-diffusion trajectories. The NPS support for the laser has had indirect impacts across a vast range of complementary technologies, including many of those reviewed in this study and many others.

6 Summary

Studies of the location of R&D, inventions, and innovations typically give heavy weight to the FPS and much less to the NPS. Rather than studying where R&D, inventions and innovations are located, we have studied the sources of the finance without which these activities could not have taken place. This greatly increases the weight attached to the NPS while reducing somewhat that of the FPS.

Success has been achieved by NPS financing in several of the technologies we have reviewed. In some cases, it seems likely that NPS support was necessary, at least initially, to kick-start the development trajectories. In other cases, development had to be initiated by the FPS before the NPS became interested in the technology. In many cases, NPS interest arose because of NEOs associated with military or political objectives. Yet in all cases, NPS support resulted in the creation and exploitation of many technological complementarities which enabled many economic opportunities and spillovers.

We see three overarching lesson from our research. First, NPS support seems to have been important (in some cases necessary) in the direct development of specific trajectories of the major technologies of the nineteenth and twentieth centuries to which it was applied. Second, NPS financing seems to work best in combination (cooperation rather than competition) with FPS support. Third, NPS financing has often generated massive technological complementarities among the many technologies on which it had direct and indirect impact. These technological complementarities have created economic spillovers in the form of opportunities for commercial success by FPS entities investing in and developing them.

Indeed, we find in the cases we have studied, particularly the more recent ones, that the activities of the NPS and the FPS are so intertwined that it makes no sense to think of turning on or off the activities of the NPS by accepting or rejecting some generic concept called 'industrial policy'.

This raises the broader issue of the successes and failures of those activities, in addition to those considered here, that come under the general heading of industrial policy. In Lipsey and Carlaw (2020), we take up this broader issue. In the first of the three main empirical sections of that paper, we summarise the results of the present Element. In the second, we consider policies designed to encourage R&D, invention, and innovation more generally. In the third, we consider policies specifically designed to pick particular winners, noting both major successes and major failures. In these three sections, we develop tentative lessons concerning the conditions favouring the success or the failure of each of the policies being considered. The paper concludes with a statement that reinforces the conclusions reached in this Element. 'The cases considered here reveal that those who would dismiss industrial policy with statements such as "Governments cannot pick winners" are relying on an empty slogan to avoid detailed consideration of the actual complicated, multifaceted relationships between the private and public sectors in encouraging the inventions and innovations that are the root of economic growth.'

Appendix: Bell Labs

Bell Laboratories originated in the late nineteenth century as the Volta Laboratory and Bureau created by Alexander Graham Bell. In 1925, it became the Bell Labs owned by the American Telephone & Telegraph Company (AT&T). Although its role was to support the monopolistic efforts of AT&T, it became what many regard as one of the most important commercial and scientific enterprises in history. By 1984, Bell Labs had amassed twenty-thousand patents, about one for each day in its existence (US Congress, Office of Technology Assessment (OTA), 1985), providing countless entrepreneurs with inventions foundational to their businesses. The scientists of Bell Labs have contributed to well-known inventions such as the laser, the transistor, UNIX, the cellular radio, and the solar cell (Bell Labs, 1993: 63), as well as a vast array of equipment provided for the army, navy and air force (Gertner, 2012: 157). On top of practical inventions, Bell has, from its inception, made contributions to pure science. For example, in 1937, Clive Davisson won a Nobel Prize for demonstrating the wave nature of matter. As recently as 2011, Bell Labs had more Nobel Prizes associated with it than any other corporation (Wu, 2011: 32–3).

Initially, Bell Labs was entirely funded by AT&T and its entities. It received steady funding even during the Great Depression. While most universities were crippled and teaching positions impossible to obtain, Bell Labs was still able to make offers and hired many of the scientists who would later be responsible for Bell's most famous inventions. These men included William Shockley, Jim Fisk, John Pierce, William Baker, and Charles Townes (Gertner, 2012: 36–9).

Stability of funding also meant that the scientists at Bell Labs could undertake long-term projects without spending time seeking research grants. While this allowed them to perform cutting-edge research in various fields, there were downsides to working for a monopolistic organisation such as AT&T. For example, in 1935, Clarence Hickman invented the answering machine only to have it suppressed for fear the invention would cause people to make fewer phone calls, thereby resulting in a loss in revenue (Wu, 2011: 31–3). Between 1936 and 1940, AT&T was investigated for monopolistic practices. Although the resulting report was generally unflattering, it did note that Bell Labs had made several important contributions to pure science (Gertner, 2012: 45).

During World War II, Bell Laboratories received more than two thousand military contracts, support that did not cease when the war ended. Between 1949 and 1959, about half of the Lab's research budget came from the US government (Lojek, 2007: 11). It was also not uncommon for Bell employees to be given leave to work on military projects. While this policy often left Bell Labs without its brightest scientists, it provided free training and important government allies.

There does not seem to be any evidence that the scientists of Bell Labs were pressured to accept government contracts against their wishes. For example, in the 1950s, Bell declined to take part in the ADVENT satellite programme, arguing that the proposed satellite was too complicated (Gertner, 2012: 210). The government proceeded without Bell Labs, but the resulting satellites were indeed too complicated and the programme was cancelled in 1962. Around the same time, NASA agreed to launch Bell's own satellite, Telstar I, on a cost-reimbursement basis and it became the first orbiting communications satellite (NASA, 2010). Bell Labs was at its largest at this time, employing about fifteen thousand people, including about twelve hundred PhDs (Gertner, 2012: 1). Bell Labs seemed unharmed by the 1985 regulation requiring it to license any patents to any applicant for a small fee (US Congress, OTA, 1985: 114).

In 1982, AT&T faced an antitrust suit that fundamentally changed the structure of the Lab. AT&T was reduced to one fourth of its size (US Congress, OTA, 1985: 111–17). The centralised Bell Labs was split into seven companies and was no longer supported by AT&T (Bell Labs, 1993: 63). The laboratories then became focussed on maximising profits for stockholders and the inventions that resulted were no longer basic underpinnings of technological advance. Funding dwindled and Bell Labs could no longer offer better salaries than universities. In 2005, one of Bell's two main campuses was shut down and its fifty-five hundred employees were laid off. The size of the other campus, the Murray Hill Complex, was severely reduced. The same year, Bell only had four scientists working on basic physics (Gertner, 2012: 331–8).

This reduction in size did not cause all innovation to cease; three of seven Nobel Prizes were received after 1984. At the beginning of the 2000s, current priorities had shifted towards producing inventions as quickly as possible, rather than creating those of the highest quality (Robertson, 2012: 38). Yet in 2009, Willard Boyle and George Smith were awarded the Nobel Prize in Physics for the invention and development of the charge-coupled device.

Then, in 2013, yet another change in direction occurred. The newly appointed president of Bell Labs stated the intention of returning the Lab to the forefront of innovation in information and communications technology, focussing on solving the key industry challenges, as was the case in the great Bell Labs innovation eras in the past. In July 2014, Bell Labs announced it had broken 'the broadband Internet speed record' with a new technology dubbed XG-FAST that promised

10 gigabits per second connectivity speeds. In 2014, Eric Betzig shared the Nobel Prize in Chemistry for his work in super-resolved fluorescence microscopy, which he began to pursue while at Bell Labs in its Semiconductor Physics Research Department. In 2015, Nokia acquired Alcatel-Lucent, Bell Labs' parent company. In 2016, Nokia Bell Labs, along with Technische Universität Berlin, Deutsche Telekom T-Labs, and the Technical University of Munich, achieved a data rate of one terabit per second by improving transmission capacity and spectral efficiency. In 2018, Arthur Ashkin shared the Nobel Prize in Physics for his work on 'the optical tweezers and their application to biological systems' originally developed at Bell Labs in the 1980s.

References

Abbate, J. (2000) *Inventing the Internet*. Cambridge: MIT Press.

Arrow, K. (1962) Economic Welfare and the Allocation of Resources for Invention, in *The Rate and Direction of Inventive Activity: Economic and Social Factors*. Cambridge, MA: National Bureau of Economic Research, pp. 609–26.

Atherton, W. A. (1984) *From Compass to Computer: A History of Electrical and Electronics Engineering*. London: MacMillan.

Aupperle, E. M. (1998) Merit: Who, What and Why, Part One: The Early Years, 1964–1983, *Library Hi Tech*, 16(1), pp. 15–36.

Barber, H. L. (1917) *Story of the Automobile, Its History and Development from 1760 to 1917: With an Analysis of the Standing and Prospects of the Automobile Industry*. Chicago: A. J. Munson & Company. http://catalog .hathitrust.org/Record/001619815

Bassett, R. K. (2002) *To the Digital Age*. Baltimore, MD: Johns Hopkins University Press.

Bedell, F., and C. A. Pierce (1928) *Direct and Alternating Current Manual: With Directions for Testing and a Discussion of the Theory of Electrical Apparatus*. 2nd ed. New York: D. Van Nostrand.

Befani, B., and J. Mayne (2018) Process Tracing and Contribution Analysis: A Combined Approach to Generative Causal Inference for Impact Evaluation, *IDS Bulletin*, 45(6), pp. 17–36.

Bell Labs. (n.d.) List of Awards. www.bell-Bell Labs.com/about/awards.html

Bell Labs. (1993) Products before Prizes *Fortune Magazine*, 127(10), p. 63.

Bellis, M. (2018) Biography of Nicolaus Otto and the Modern Engine, ThoughtCo, 6 December. thoughtco.com/nicolaus-otto-engine-design-4072867

Berners-Lee, T. (2010) What Were the First WWW Browsers? World Wide Web Consortium (W3C). www.w3.org/DesignIssues/TimBook-old/History.html

Bertolotti, M. (2004) *The History of the Laser*. Boca Raton, FL: CRC Press.

Bloomfield, G. (1978) *The World Automotive Industry*. North Pomfret, VT: David & Charles.

Bluhm, R. K. (1958) Remarks on the Royal Society's Finances 1660–1768, *Notes and Records of the Royal Society*, 13, pp. 103–82.

Boldrin, M., and D. K. Levine (2008) *Against Intellectual Monopoly*. Cambridge: Cambridge University Press.

Bourne, J. (1852) *A Treatise on the Screw Propeller with Various Suggestions for Improvement*. London: Longman, Brown, Green and Longmans.

Bowen, J. (2010) *The Economic Geography of Air Transportation*. New York: Routledge.

British North American Database, 1758–1867 (1852) An Act to Establish a Consolidated Municipal Loan Fund for Upper Canada, 10th November 1852, *Upper Canada, 16 Victoria*, chapter 22. https://bnald.lib .unb.ca/legislation/act-establish-consolidated-municipal-loan-fund-upper-canada-10th-november-1852

Bromberg, J. L. (1986) The Birth of the Laser, *Physics Today*, 41(10), pp. 26–33.

Bromberg, J. L. (1991) *The Laser in America, 1950–1970*. Cambridge, MA: MIT Press.

Bromley, A. G. (1990) Difference and Analytical Engines, in W. Aspray (ed.), *Computing before Computers*. Ames: Iowa State University Press, pp. 59–98.

Brooks, P. W. (1967) The Development of Air Transport, *Journal of Transport Economics and Policy*, 1(2), pp. 164–83.

Brown, D. C. (1980) *Electricity for Rural America: The Fight for REA*. Westport, CT: Greenwood Press.

Brunel, I. (1870) *The Life of Isambard Kingdom Brunel, Civil Engineer*. London: Longmans, Green and Company.

Burton, A. (1980) *The Rainhill Story*. London: British Broadcasting Corporation.

Buttel, F. H., M. Kenney, and J. Kloppenburg (1985) From Green Revolution to Biorevolution: Some Observations on the Changing Technological Bases of Economic Transformation in the Third World, *Economic Development and Cultural Change*, 34(1), pp. 31–55.

Caliskan, O. (2010) An Analysis of the Airbus-Boeing Dispute from the Perspective of the WTO Process, *EGE Academic Review*, 10(4), pp. 1129–1238.

Campbell-Kelly, M., and W. Aspray (1996) *Computers, Data Gathering, Internet, Computer: A History of the Information Machine*. New York: Martin Basic Books.

Carlaw, K. I., and R. G. Lipsey (2002) Externalities, Technological Complementarities and Sustained Economic Growth, *Research Policy*, 31 (8–9), pp. 1305–15.

Carlaw, K. I., R. G. Lipsey, and R. Webb (2007) Has the ICT Revolution Run Its Course? Simon Fraser University Department of Economics Working Paper Series, dp07-18.

Casserley, H. C. (1960) *Historic Locomotive Pocket Book*. London: Batsford.

Ceruzzi, P. E. (2003) *A History of Modern Computing*. Cambridge, MA: MIT Press.

Chandler, A. D. (1977) *The Visible Hand: The Managerial Revolution in American Business*. Cambridge, MA: Harvard University Press.

Chandler, A. D. (1990) *Scale and Scope: The Dynamics of Industrial Capitalism*. Cambridge, MA: The Belknap Press of Harvard University Press.

Channon, G. (1981) The Great Western Railway under the British Railways Act of 1921. *The Business History Review*, 55(2), pp. 188–216.

Chisholm, H., ed. (1922). Zeppelin, Count Ferdinand von. *Encyclopædia Britannica* (12th ed.). London and New York: The Encyclopædia Britannica Company.

Clark, L. A. (1976) *North of the Harbour: A Brief History of Transport to and on the North Shore*. Alexandria, NSW: Australian Railway Historical Society.

Cochrane, W. W. (1993) *The Development of American Agriculture: A Historical Analysis*. Minneapolis: University of Minnesota Press.

Comer, D. (1983) History and Overview of CSNET. *Communications*, 26(10), pp. 747–53.

Conway, E. M. (2005) *High-Speed Dreams: NASA and the Technopolitics of Supersonic Transportation, 1945–1999*, Baltimore, MD: Johns Hopkins University Press.

Cootner, P. H. (1963) The Role of the Railroads in United States Economic Growth. *The Journal of Economic History*, 23(4), pp. 477–521.

Corlett, E. (1975) *The Iron Ship: The Story of Brunel's SS* Great Britain. London: Conway.

Crump, T. (2007) *A Brief History of the Age of Steam: From the First Engine to the Boats and Railways*. Philadelphia, PA: Running Press.

Currie, A. W. (1957) *The Grand Trunk Railway of Canada*. Toronto: University of Toronto Press.

Day, J. (2009) Beyond the Bar Code: New Tech Helps Shoppers Identify Everything from a Product's Origins to Its Allergen Content, *Natural Foods Merchandiser Magazine*, 30(9), p. 554.

de Syon, Guillaume (2001) *Zeppelin: Germany and the Airship, 1900–1939*. Baltimore, MD: Johns Hopkins University Press.

Dee, R. (2007) *The Man Who Discovered Flight: George Cayley and the First Airplane*. Toronto: McClelland and Stewart, pp. 86–7.

Deng, Y. (2005) *Ancient Chinese Inventions*. Beijing: China Intercontinental Press.

Donaghy, T. J. (1966) The Liverpool and Manchester Railway As an Investment, *Journal of Transport History*, 7(4), pp. 225–33.

Dooley, S. C. (2004) The Development of Material-Adapted Structural Form. Part II: Appendices, THÈSE NO 2986. École Polytechnique Fédérale de Lausanne.

DuBoff, R. (1980) Business Demand and the Development of the Telegraph in the United States, 1844–1860, *Business History Review*, 54, pp. 461–77.

Dudley, L. (1991) *The Word and the Sword: How the Technologies of Information and Violence Have Shaped Our World*. Cambridge, MA: Basil Blackwell.

Fabrizio, K. R., and D. Mowery (2007) The Federal Role in Financing Major Innovations: Information Technology during the Post War Period, in N. R. Lamoreaux and K. L Sokoloff (eds.), *Financing Innovation in the United States, 1870 to Present*. Cambridge, MA: MIT Press Scholarship Online, pp. 283–316. https://doi-org.eu1.proxy.openathens.net/10.7551/mit press/9780262122894.001.0001

Federal Aviation Administration. (1997) Airport Privatization Pilot Program. www.faa.gov/airports/airport_compliance/privatization

Federal Aviation Administration (2012) Fact Sheet: What Is the Airport Privatization Pilot Program? June 29. www.faa.gov/news/fact_sheets/news_story.cfm?newsId=13333

Fishlow, A. (1966) Productivity and Technological Change in the Railroad Sector, 1840–1910, in Output, Employment, and Productivity in the United States after 1800, *National Bureau of Economic Research, Studies in Income and Wealth*, 30, pp. 583–646.

Fitzgerald-Moore. P., and B. J. Parai (1996) The Green Revolution. Unpublished. www.yumpu.com/en/document/view/27430970/the-green-revolution-university-of-calgary

Flamm, K. (1988) *Creating the Computer*. Washington, DC: Brookings Institute.

Fletcher, A. M. (2012) Two Blades of Grass: The Role of Science in the Green Revolution, *Juniata Voices*, 12, pp. 20–6.

Gamst, F. C. (1992) The Context and Significance of America's First Railroad, on Boston's Beacon Hill. *Technology and Culture*, 33(1), pp. 66–100.

Gee, B. (1993) The Early Development of the Magneto-electric Machine. *Annals of Science*, 50, p. 101.

Geiges, L. M. (2011) History of Lasers in Dermatology. *Basics in Dermatological Laser Applications*, 4, pp. 1–6.

Gertner, J. (2012) *The Idea Factory: Bell Labs and the Great Age of American Innovation*. New York: Penguin.

Gibson, A. F., M. F. Kimmitt, and A. C. Walker (1970) Photon Drag in Germanium. *Applied Physics Letters*, 17(2), pp. 75–7.

Glab, J. (2003) Air France: 70 Years of Innovation, Elegance and Style. *Air Transport World*, Special Edition, pp. 80–5.

Golich, V. L., and T. E. Pinelli (1997) The Influence of U.S. Public Policy on Large Commercial Aircraft: Innovation, Transportation, and Knowledge Diffusion, in T. E. Pinelli, R. O. Barclay, J. M. Kennedy, and A. P. Bishop (eds.), *Knowledge Diffusion in the U.S. Aerospace Industry: Managing Knowledge for Competitive Advantage*. Greenwich, CT: Ablex, pp. 35–84.

Grosz, P. M., G. Haddow, and P. Schiemer (1993) *Austro-Hungarian Army Aircraft of World War One*. Boulder, CO: Flying Machines Press.

GS1 (2016) *GS1 GPC Standards December 2016*. www.gs1.org/standards/gpc/dec-2016

Hall, M. B. (1981). Public Science in Britain: The Role of the Royal Society. *Isis*, 72(4), pp. 627–9.

Hallion, R. P. (2003) *Taking Flight: Inventing the Aerial Age from Antiquity through the First World War*. Oxford: Oxford University Press.

Harwood, C. S., and G. B. Fogel (2012) *Quest for Flight: John J. Montgomery and the Dawn of Aviation in the West*. Oklahoma: University of Oklahoma Press.

Hazell, P. B. R. (2009) Transforming Agriculture: The Green Revolution in Asia, in D. J. Spielman and R. Pandya-Lorch (eds.), *Millions Fed: Proven Successes in Agricultural Development*. Washington, DC: International Food Policy Research Institute, pp. 25–32.

Heavisides, M. (1912) *The History of the First Public Railway (Stockton & Darlington)*. Self Published.

Hecht, J. (2005) *Beam: The Race to Make the Laser*. Oxford: Oxford University Press.

Hecht, J. (2010) The First Half-Century of Laser Development. *Laser Technik Journal*, 7(4), pp. 20–5.

Heitmann, J. A. (2009) *The Automobile and American Life*. Jefferson, NC: McFarland.

Herapath, J. (1839) *The Railway Magazine and Steam Navigation Journal, VI*. London: James Wyld

Hijiya, J. A. (1973) Making a Railroad: The Political Economy of the Ithaca and Owego, 1828–1842. *New York History*, 54(2), pp. 145–73.

Hoddeson, L., and V. Dautch (2002) *True Genius: The Life and Science of John Bardeen*. Washington, DC: National Academy Press.

Hood, C. P. (2006). *Shinkansen: From Bullet Train to Symbol of Modern Japan*. New York: Routledge.

Hopcroft, J. E. (1984) Turing Machines. *Scientific American*, 250(5), pp. 86–98.

Hoshino, T., and H. Seko (1996) History of Wheat Breeding for a Half Century in Japan. *Euphytica*, 89(2), pp. 215–21.

Hunter, L. C. (1985) *A History of Industrial Power in the United States 1730–1930*, vol. 2: *Steam Power*. Charlottesville: University of Virginia Press.

Jones, M. (2012) *Lancashire Railways: The History of Steam*. Newbury: Countryside Books, p. 5.

KAMA. (2005) *Fifty Years of Korea's Automobile Industry*. KAMA

Kenworthy, L. (1995) *In Search of National Economic Success: Balancing Competition and Cooperation*. Thousand Oaks, CA: Sage.

Key, M. (2006) *Adventures in Laser Produced Plasma Research*. https://e-reports-ext.llnl.gov/pdf/329367.pdf

Kim, B.-K. (2005) *Internationalising the Internet: The Co-evolution of Influence and Technology*. Cheltenham: Edward Elgar.

King, P. (2010) The First Shropshire Railways, in G. Boyes (ed.), *Early Railways 4: Papers from the 4th International Early Railways Conference 2008*. Sudbury: Six Marlets, pp. 70–84.

Kleinrock, L., B. Kahn, and D. Clark (1988) *Toward a National Research Network*. Washington DC: National Academy Press.

Kleint, C. (1998) Julius Edgar Lilienfeld: Life and Profession, *Progress in Surface Science*, 57(4), pp. 253–328.

Klepper, S. (2007) The Organizing and Financing of Innovative Companies in the Evolution of the U.S. Automobile Industry, in N. R. Lamoreaux and K. L. Sokoloff (eds.), *Financing Innovation in the United States, 1870 to the Present*. Cambridge, MA: MIT Press, pp. 85–126. http://site.ebrary.com/lib/ubc/docDetail.action?docID=10173595

Langlois, R., and D. Mowery (1996) Spinning Off and Spinning On(?): The Federal Government Role in the Development of the US Computer Software Industry. *Research Policy*, 25(6), pp. 947–66.

Lawrence, P. K., and D. W. Thornton (2005) *Deep Stall: The Turbulent Story of Boeing Commercial Airplanes*. Burlington, VT: Ashgate.

Lee, A. I., and J. S. Mah (2017) The Role of the Government in the Development of the Automobile Industry in Korea. *Progress in Development Studies*, 17(3), pp. 229–34.

Lipsey, R. G. (2013) Some Contentious Issues in Theory and Policy in Memory of Mark Blaug, in M. Boumans and M. Klaes (eds.), *Mark Blaug: Rebel with Many Causes*. Cheltenham: Edward Elgar, pp. 31–62.

Lipsey, R. G., and K. I. Carlaw (2020) Industrial Policies: Common Not Rare. Simon Fraser Economics Department Discussion Paper dp20-11.

Lipsey, R. G., and K. I. Carlaw (1996) A Structuralist View of Innovation Policy, in P. Howitt (ed.), *The Implications of Knowledge Based Growth*. Calgary: University of Calgary Press, pp. 255–333.

Lipsey, R. G., K. I. Carlaw, and C. T. Bekar (2005) *Economic Transformations: General Purpose Technologies and Long Run Growth*. Oxford: Oxford University Press.

Lipsey, R. G., and K. Lancaster (1958) The General Theory of Second Best. *The Review of Economic Studies*, 24(1),11–32.

Lojek, B. (2007) *History of Semiconductor Engineering*. London: Springer.

Lowe, J. W. (1989) *British Steam Locomotive Builders*. London: Guild.

Lucas, R. E. (1988) On the Mechanics of Economic Growth. *Journal of Monetary Economics*, 22(1), pp. 3–42.

Loundon, R., and E. G. S. Paige (1991) Alan Frank Gibson 30 May 1923–27 March 1988. *Biographical Memoirs of the Fellows of the Royal Society*, 37, pp. 221–44.

Lukasiewicz, J. (1976) *The Railway Game*. Toronto: McGill-Queen's Press.

Maat, H. (2011) The History and Future of Agricultural Experiments. *NJAS: Wageningen Journal of Life Sciences*, 57(3–4), pp. 187–95.

Macassey, L. (1922) The Railways Act, 1921. *Journal of Comparative Legislation and International Law, Third Series*, 4 (4), pp. 162–75.

Mackie, P., and N. Smith (2005) Financing Roads in Great Britain. *Research in Transportation Economics*, 15, pp. 215–29.

Magoun, F. A., and E. Hodgins (1931) *A History of Aircraft*. New York: Whittlesey House.

Mansfield, H. (1966) *Vision: The Story of Boeing: A Aaga of the Sky and New Horizons of Space*. New York: Duell Sloan and Pearce.

Markusen, A. (2000) Can Technology Policy Serve As Industrial Policy? in C. Howes and A. Singh (eds.), *Industry and Economic Performance in the U. S.* Ann Arbor: University of Michigan Press.

Marsh, J. (2009) Railway History. *The Canadian Encyclopedia*. www.thecana dianencyclopedia.ca/en/article/railway-history

McDougall, J. L. (1968) *Canadian Pacific: A Brief History*. Montreal: McGill University Press.

McFarland, M. W. (ed.) (1953) *The Papers of Wilbur and Orville Wright, including the Chanute-Wright Letters and Other Papers of Octave Chanute*. New York: McGraw-Hill.

McMahon, A. M. (1984) *The Making of a Profession: A Century of Electrical Engineering in America*. New York: IEEE Press.

McNeil, I. (2002) *An Encyclopedia of the History of Technology*. New York: Routledge.

McNeill, D. (2010) Behind the 'Heathrow Hassle': A political and cultural economy of the privatized airport. *Environment and Planning*, 42, pp. 2859–73.

Mercer, L. J. (1982) *Railroad and Land Grant Policy: Study in Government Intervention*. New York: Academic Press.

Mindell, D. (2008) *Digital Apollo: Human and Machine in Spaceflight*. Cambridge, MA: MIT Press.

Morison, J. H. (1903) *History of American Steam Navigation*. New York: Sametz and Company.

Mowery, D. (1988) *The Impact of Technological Change on Employment and Economic Growth: Papers Commissioned by the Panel on Technology and Employment*. Cambridge, MA: Harper and Row, pp. 481–509.

Mowery, D. (1991) International Collaboration in the Commercial Aircraft Industry, in L. K. Mytelka (ed.), *Strategic Partnerships and the World Economy*. London: Pinter, pp. 78–101.

National Aeronautics and Space Administration (NASA) (2010) *Communications Satellite Short History*. http://history.nasa.gov/printFriendly/satcomhistory.html

National Research Council Staff (NRCS) (1999) *Funding a Revolution: Government Support for Computing Research. U.S. National Research Council Committee on Innovations in Computing and Communications: Lessons from History*. Washington, DC: National Academies Press. http://site.ebrary.com/lib/ubc/Doc?id=10041036

Nelson, R., and S. Winter (1982) *An Evolutionary Theory of Economic Change*. Cambridge, MA: Harvard University Press.

O'Regan, G. (2008) *A Brief History of Computing*. London: Springer.

Peng, S., and G. Khush (2003) Four Decades of Breeding for Varietal Improvement of Irrigated Lowland Rice in the International Rice Research Institute. *Plant Production Science*, 6(3), pp. 157–64.

Petersen, J. K. (2002) *FiberOptics Illustrated Dictionary*. Boca Raton, FL: CRC Press, Taylor Francis Group.

Pire, B. (2018) Leclanché Georges (1839–1882). *Encyclopædia Universalis* [online]. www.universalis.fr/encyclopedie/georges-leclanche

Pokrovsky, V. (2013) Russian Academy of Sciences Elects Reformer As President. *Science*. www.sciencemag.org/news/2013/05/russian-academy-sciences-elects-reformer-president

Pollins, H. (1952) The Finances of the Liverpool and Manchester Railway. *Economic History Review*, 5(1), pp. 90–7.

Previts, G. J., and W. D. Samson (2000) Exploring the Contents of the Baltimore and Ohio Railroad Annual Reports: 1827–1856. *The Accounting Historians Journal*, 27(1), pp.1–42.

Pumfrey, S. (2002) *Latitude and the Magnetic Earth*. London: Icon Books.

Quin-Harkin, A. J. (1954) Imperial Airways, 1920–40. *Journal of Transportation History*, 1(4), pp. 197–215.

Rae, J. (1905) *The Sociological Theory of Capital, Being a Complete Reprint of the New Principles of Political Economy, 1834*, ed. C. W. Mixter. New York: Macmillan.

Rao, A., and P. Scaruffi (2013) The Lab Magicians (Chapter 4), in *A History of Silicon Valley*. Omniware Group.

Regehr, T. D. (2006) Canadian Northern Railway. *The Canadian Encyclopedia*. www.thecanadianencyclopedia.ca/en/article/canadian-northern-railway

Regehr, T. D. (1972) Serving the Canadian West: Policies and Problems of the Canadian Northern Railway. *Western Historical Quarterly*, 3(3), pp. 283–98.

Reid, J. (1886) *The Telegraph in America*. New York: Polhemus.

The Repertory of Patent Inventions: And Other Discoveries and Improvements in Arts, Manufactures, and Agriculture; Being a Continuation, On an Enlarged Plan, of the Repertory of Arts & Manufactures (1825) London: Published for the proprietors by T. and G. Underwood.

Reynolds, M., and N. Borlaug (2006) Impacts of Breeding on International Collaborative Wheat Improvement. *The Journal of Agricultural Science*, pp. 3–17.

Rice, V. E. (1978) The Arizona Agricultural Experiment Station: A History to 1917. *Arizona and the West*, 22(2), pp. 123–40.

Riordan, M. (2004) *The Lost History of the Transistor*. New York: IEEE Spectrum.

Robertson, D. (2012) Spend Millions on Top-Secret Research, then Share It with the Rest of the World: AT&T Opens the Door on Its latest Innovations. *Times* (London), 38. http://global.factiva.com/ha/default.aspx

Robinson, G. S., and C. Cargill (1996) History and Impact of Computer Standards. *Computer*, 29(10), pp. 79–85.

Romer, P. (1990) Endogenous Technological Change. *Journal of Political Economy*, 98(5), pp. S71–S102.

Rose, M. H., and R. A. Mohl (2012) *Interstate: Highway Politics and Policy since 1939*. Third edition. Knoxville: University of Tennessee Press.

Rosenberg, N. (1994) *Exploring the Black Box: Technology, Economic, History*. Cambridge: Cambridge University Press.

Rosenberg, N. (1982) *Inside the Black Box: Technology and Economics*, Cambridge: Cambridge University Press.

Rosenberg, N. (1963) Technological Change in the Machine Tool Industry, 1840–1910. *The Journal of Economic History*, 23(4), pp. 414–43.

Rosenberg, N. (1996) Uncertainty and Technological Change, in R. Landau, T. Taylor, and G. Wright (eds.) *The Mosaic of Economic Growth*. Stanford, CA: Stanford University Press.

Rural Electrification Administration (REA), US Dept. of Agriculture (1966) USA: The Story of Cooperative Rural Electrification. Originally published in *Rural Lines*, Oct. 1959. Miscellaneous Publication no. 811. Washington, DC, p. 48.

Ruttan, V. W. (2001) *Technology, Growth, and Development: An Induced Innovativation Perspective*. New York: Oxford University Press.

SAGE (2005) Semi-Automatic Ground Environment (SAGE). MITRE. www .mitre.org/about/sage.html

Saloutos, T. (1982) *The American Farmer and the New Deal*. Ames: Iowa State University Press.

Sarkar, J. G., G. Khan, and A. Basumallick (2007) Nanowires: Properties, Applications and Synthesis via Porous Anodic Aluminium Oxide Template. *Bulletin of Material Science*, 30(3), pp. 271–90.

Savage, C. (2006) *Economic History of Transport in Britain*. New York: Routledge.

Schewe, P. F. (2007) *The Grid: A Journey through the Heart of Our Electrified World*. Washington, DC: Joseph Henry Press.

Schnaars, S. (1994) *Managing Imitation Strategies: How Later Entrants Seize Markets from Pioneers*. New York: The Free Press.

Schumpeter, J. (1942) *Capitalism, Socialism, and Democracy*. New York: Harper & Bros.

Schuster, J. (2016) A Brief History of Internet Service Providers. 10 June. https://corpblog.viasat.com

Science and Industry Museum (2018) www.scienceandindustrymuseum.org .uk/objects-and-stories/making-the-liverpool-and-manchester-railway

Scott, P. (1995) Birth of the Jet Engine. *Mechanical Engineering*, 116(1), pp. 66–71.

Scottish Optoelectronics Association (2010) *50 Years of Lasers in Scotland*. Scottish Optoelectronics Association. www.sdi.co.uk/resources/brochures/ ict-and-electronic-technologies/50-years-of-lasers-in-scotland.aspx

Seifer, M. J. (1988) *Wizard: The Life and Times of Nikola Tesla*. New York: Citadel Press.

Schlesinger, H. (2010) *The Battery: How Portable Power Sparked a Technological Revolution*. New York: Harper Collins.

Shampo, M. A., R. A. Kyle, and D. P. Steensma (2012) Nikolay Basov: Nobel Prize for Lasers and Masers. *Mayo Clinic Proceedings*, p. e3.

Simonson, G. R. (1960) The demand for aircraft and the aircraft industry, 1907–1958. *The Journal of Economic History*, 20(3), pp. 361–82.

Slattery, H. (1940) *Rural America Lights Up*. Washington, DC: National Home Library Foundation.

Spetz, J. (1995) Physicians and Physicists: The Interdisciplinary Introduction of the Laser to Medicine, in N. Rosenberg, A. C. Gelijns, and H. Dawkins (eds.), *Sources of medical technology: Universities and industry.* Washington, DC: National Academies Press. www.ncbi.nlm.nih.gov/book/NBK232041

Spitzer, P. (2004) Boeing As a Start-Up Company, 1915–1917. *The Pacific Northwest Quarterly*, 95(3), pp. 140–8.

Swann, L. A. (1965) *John Roach, Maritime Entrepreneur: The Years As Naval Contractor 1862–1886.* Washington, DC: United States Naval Institute.

Thévenot, R. (1979) *A History of Refrigeration throughout the World*, trans. J. C. Fidler. Paris: International Institute of Refrigeration.

Thiesen, W. H. (2006) *Industrializing American Shipbuilding: The Transformation of Ship Design and Construction, 1820–1920.* Gainesville: University Press of Florida.

Thompson, W. R. (2004) Complexity, Diminishing Marginal Returns and Serial Mesopotamian Fragmentation. *Journal of World-Systems Research*, 10(3), 613–52.

Thuong, L. T. (1982) Government Railroading, Japanese Style. *Transportation Journal*, 22(2), pp. 21–31.

Todd, D., and J. Simpson (1986) *The World Aircraft Industry.* Massachusetts: Auburn House.

Tribe, D. (1994) *Feeding and Greening the World: The Role of International Agricultural Research.* Wallingford, UK: CAB International.

Trischler, H., and S. Zeilinger (eds.) (2003) *Tackling Transport*, vol. 3 of The Artefacts Series – Studies in the History of Science and Technology. NMSI Trading Ltd.

Tucker, A. (2009) Canadian National Railway (CN). *The Canadian Encyclopedia.* www.thecanadianencyclopedia.ca/en/article/canadian-national-railways

Turing, A. (1936) On Computable Numbers with an Application to the Entscheidungs Problem. Proceedings of the London Mathematical Society.

US Congress, Office of Technology Assessment (OTA) (1985) *Information Technology and R & D: Critical Trends and Issues.* http://ota-cdn.fas.org/reports/8511.pdf

US Congress, Session 3 of the 75th Congress (1938) The Civil Aviation Act 1938, in *U.S. Statutes at Large*, Vol. 52, pp. 973–1030.

van Dormael, A. (2009) Biographies: Herbert A Mataré, *IEEE Annals of Computing History*, (IEEE Computer Society). https://ieeexplore.ieee.org/stamp/stamp.jsp?arnumber=5223988

Van Dormael, A. (2013) *The 'French' Transistor.* www.cdvandt.org/VanDormael.pdf

Waite, B. P. (1962) *The Life and Times of Confederation 1864–1867*. Toronto: University of Toronto Press.

Weiss, E. (1996) Konrad Zuse 1919–1995. *IEEE Annals of the History of Computing*, 18(2), pp. 3–5.

Wensveen, J. G. (2007) *Air Transportation: A Management Perspective*. Sixth edition. Burlington, VT: Ashgate.

Wheeland, R. G. (1995) Clinical Uses of Lasers in Dermatology. *Lasers in Surgery and Medicine*, 16(1), pp. 2–23.

Winston, B. (1998) *Media Technology and Society*. New York: Routledge.

Womack, J. P., D. T. Jones, and D. Roos (1990) *The Machine That Changed the World: Based on the Massachusetts Institute of Technology 5-Million-Dollar 5-Year Study on the Future of the Automobile*. New York: Rawson Associates.

Wright, R. (2004) *A Short History of Progress*. Toronto: House of Anansi Press.

Wu, T. (2011) Bell Labs and Centralized Innovation. *Communications of the AGM*, 54(5), pp. 31–3.

Yorke, S. (2007) *Steam Railways Explained: Steam, Oil & Locomotion*. Newbury: Countryside Books.

Zadoks, J. (2003) Fifty Years of Crop Protection, 1950–2000. *NJAS: Wageningen Journal of Life Sciences*, 181–93.

Cambridge Elements ☰

Evolutionary Economics

John Foster
University of Queensland

John Foster is Emeritus Professor of Economics at the University of Queensland, Brisbane. He is Fellow of the Academy of Social Science in Australia; Life member of Clare Hall College, Cambridge; and Past President of the International J. A. Schumpeter Society. He is also Director of the Energy Economics and Management Group at UQ and Focal Leader for Renewable Energy at the Global Change Institute.

Jason Potts
RMIT Univeristy

Jason Potts is Professor of Economics at RMIT University, Melbourne. He is also an Adjunct Fellow at the Institute of Public Affairs. His research interests include technological change, economics of innovation, and economics of cities. He was the winner of the 2000 International Joseph A. Schumpeter Prize and has published over sixty articles and six books.

About the Series

The Cambridge Elements of Evolutionary Economics provides authoritative and up-to-date reviews of core topics and recent developments in the field. It includes state-of-the-art contributions on all areas in the field. The series is broadly concerned with questions of dynamics and change, with a particular focus on processes of entrepreneurship and innovation, industrial and institutional dynamics, and on patterns of economic growth and development.

Cambridge Elements ☰

Evolutionary Economics